A PEOPLE'S MEDICAL SOCIETY BOOK

Take
This Book
to the
Gynecologist
with You

A CONSUMER'S GUIDE TO WOMEN'S HEALTH

Gale Maleskey and Charles B. Inlander

Addison-Wesley Publishing Company, Inc.
Reading, Massachusetts   Menlo Park, California   New York
Don Mills, Ontario   Wokingham, England   Amsterdam   Bonn
Sydney   Singapore   Tokyo   Madrid   San Juan
Paris   Seoul   Milan   Mexico City   Taipei

Many of the designations used by manufacturers and sellers to distinguish their products are claimed as trademarks. Where those designations appear in this book and Addison-Wesley was aware of a trademark claim, the designations have been printed in initial capital letters (e.g., Nilstat).

Library of Congress Cataloging-in-Publication Data

Maleskey, Gale.
   Take this book to the gynecologist with you : a consumer's guide
to women's health / Gale Maleskey and Charles B. Inlander.
     p.   cm.
   "A People's Medical Society book."
   Includes bibliographical references and index.
   ISBN 0-201-52379-5
   1. Gynecology—Popular works. 2. Women—Medical examinations.
3. Consumer education. I. Inlander, Charles B. II. Title.
RG121.M32   1991
618.1—dc20   90-23365
                                                  CIP

Cover design by Hannus Design Associates
Text design by Jennie Bush, Designworks, Inc.
Set in 10-point ITC Bookman by DEKR Corporation, Woburn, MA

1 2 3 4 5 6 7 8 9 10 MA 9594939291
First printing, May 1991

Contents

Preface

You may not think of yourself in such a businesslike fashion, but as a woman, you are part of "the most exciting market segment in medicine today." Those words, from one gynecologist/business entrepreneur, reflect a hard-nosed fact: Out of women's pocketbooks come the bulk of health care business profits.

Women see a doctor twice as often as men, have about one-third more outpatient surgery, and are hospitalized about 15 percent more often. Operations unique to women, such as cesarean sections and hysterectomies, make up seven of the twenty most frequently performed surgeries. Women's office visits, tests, and hospital stays generate over $20 billion a year.

That's big business, and those who expect to profit from it include not only doctors but drug companies making oral contraceptives and estrogen patches, hospitals eager to fill empty beds, and medical-equipment manufacturers peddling mammography machines and carbon-dioxide lasers.

These people may be less concerned about your need for their services, or the quality with which those services are performed, than with convincing you to buy. They may hope you won't ask too many questions, that you'll simply go along with whatever is recommended to you, possibly at your body's expense. Traditionally, that's the way it's been with women and medicine.

There's no doubt that most of us are going to require at least some medical services during our lives. So doesn't it make sense to realize we *are* purchasing services, possibly from someone eager to sell to us whether we need it or not? Think of all the questions we ask when we purchase a car. What about the grilling we put a bank loan officer through when we are considering a mortgage? We ask questions of these service providers in order to learn our options—before we say yes or no. Shouldn't we be doing the same with our medical practitioners?

Wandering unknowingly into the world of medicine can be like inadvertently taking a vacation in a combat zone. It's full of hidden dangers. It's up to you, the consumer, to uncover and avoid those dangers.

Acknowledgments

All books are a collaborative effort. From the idea to the research, from the writing to the production; many highly skilled and capable people contribute to the final product. And so it is with *Take This Book to the Gynecologist with You*.

We extend our sincerest thanks and utmost gratitude to those individuals who have provided their knowledge, skill, time, and support for this project.

We begin by thanking Nancy Miller, our editor at Addison-Wesley Publishing Company, for her insight, assistance, and belief in the project. To the Addison-Wesley production crew, the unsung heroes who take a manuscript and make it readable, presentable, and useful, we express our utmost appreciation. Thanks to Jane Isay, who saw the importance of the People's Medical Society book projects four years ago.

These days there cannot be a People's Medical Society book without Gail Ross, our literary agent, PMS Board member, and friend. She is the backbone of our entire publishing program. There is nobody better.

Many physicians and health care professionals were interviewed for this book. We especially want to acknowledge and thank: Dr. Wulf Utian, director of obstetrics and gynecology at University McDonald Women's Hospital in Cleveland; Dr. Gita Gidwani, head of pediatric and adolescent gynecology at the Cleveland Clinic; Dr. Daniel Kopans, director of breast imaging at Massachusetts General Hospital, Boston; Dr. Marsha Mc-Neese, head of breast-radiotherapy at the M.D. Anderson Cancer Center in Houston; Dr. Don Gambrell, professor of obstetrics and gynecology at the Medical College of Georgia, Augusta; Dr. Timothy Johnson, director of the obstetrics and gynecology residency training program at Johns Hopkins Hospital, Baltimore; Scott Dugan of Capital Blue Cross/Blue Shield, Harrisburg, Pa.; Sue Lubbers of St. Paul Fire and Marine Insurance, Minneapolis; and, Kate Ruddon of the American College of Obstetricians and Gynecologists.

Special thanks to Gale Maleskey's mother, Sandra Maleskey, for her generous and loving support. And for their invaluable guidance, our sincerest appreciation to Maggie Spilner and Deena Balboa. Thanks also to Mary Ann Napoli and the Center for Medical Consumers in New York.

The outstanding contribution of the staff of the People's Medical Society and especially Director of Projects, Mike Donio, must be noted. Known as "Mr. Charts," Mike is responsible for the charts and forms found at the end of the book. He is also a major member of the research team. Karla Morales provided research materials, Gayle Ebert helped secure permissions where needed, and Bill Bauman did his usual fine job of bringing order to chaos.

Finally, our thanks to the tens of thousands of People's Medical Society members for whom we work and to whom this book is dedicated.

Introduction

Gynecology is the most intimate of medical specialties. A woman's relationship with her gynecologist is unique: It deals with a woman's reproductive system; the practitioners are still predominantly men; and, many of the subjects and issues that arise are often taboo in general social conversation. Based on this uniqueness, an objective observer might presume that women are knowledgeable about not only their gynecologist (if they have one), but about the ins and outs of gynecology as well. And, yet, the very same factors that make the relationship unique are precisely why most women know virtually nothing about their gynecologist, or gynecology in general.

All aspects of medicine are intimidating to the consumer. As a society we have been led to believe that the doctor is a high priest, possessing a special knowledge too complex for us mortals to understand or even dare question. Doctors intimidate us with their language, equipment, manner, and often their bravado. Hospitals are formidable bastions of intimidation with their protocols, laboratories, forms, hubbub, machinery, and cost.

Medical intimidation is the child of ignorance. As medical consumers, little is disclosed to us about the conditions we have, those who practice upon us, or the setting where medical care is delivered. We pass through medical-land as innocents, hoping we are on course, but not really knowing where we are going.

For women in the gynecological setting, this intimidation

is even more formidable. Too often a woman is forced to "strip bare" physically and emotionally to a virtual stranger. She must yield her body to probing and handling by a person she would have arrested if the setting were anything other than a medical one.

It is because of this intimidation, this lack of knowledge, that we wrote *Take This Book to the Gynecologist with You*. Its purpose is to empower you through information. Throughout the book we have attempted to pass along the vital and most updated information you need to know in order to help shape your own successful outcomes and experiences.

In 1985, we published our first People's Medical Society book. It was called *Take This Book to the Hospital with You*. It was an immediate success. Our goal was to empower the hospital consumer; to give him or her the information, questions, and knowledge needed to survive a hospital stay.

Throughout the medical world, the book caused a furor. The medical "powers that be" accused us of scaring patients. They said that giving information about such matters as hospital-caused infections, drug errors, and horrible billing practices would make consumers afraid to use hospitals. Of course, nothing could be further from the truth. In fact, because we told the truth, hundreds of thousands of consumers have had better hospital experiences. We like to think that many hospitals have changed as a result.

Our goal is the same with *Take This Book to the Gynecologist with You*. This book is designed to put you in control. It is not designed to give you the answers to everything that may medically present itself. While many questions are answered, much of what you will find in the following pages are the questions you need to ask.

In the preface to *Take This Book to the Hospital with You*, I noted that the book was written for consumers by consumers. And so it is again. Gale Maleskey and I are not doctors. We don't claim to be. To assemble this book we have reviewed the most important medical literature, in the most important medical journals. We have reviewed hundreds of studies, interviewed scores of practitioners, talked to numerous researchers, and listened to legions of women.

Our intention was to be as medically unbiased as possible.

We have no medical products to sell. We are not promoting a treatment, facility, or a group of practitioners. We think we have met our goal.

But, lo, this book does have a bias. It is biased toward the consumer. And for that we are proud.

Undoubtedly there will be some medical practitioners offended by this book. They won't like the fact that the authors were not from the gynecological inner sanctum. They will be upset by some of the topics we discuss. They will feel we are meddling, sticking our noses into their business, because we disclose to women the controversies and lack of science present in many gynecological matters.

But let them be mad at us. Don't let them take it out on you. Remember, you are the customer, and it is your body and your life that is at stake here. If your physician does not like that you *Take This Book to the Gynecologist with You*, it is probably time for you to find a new doctor.

Charles B. Inlander
President
People's Medical Society

CHAPTER ONE

Before You Go . . .

Most women believe gynecologists deal exclusively with reproductive matters and problems. Yet gynecology is defined as a branch of medicine that deals with the "diseases and hygiene of women." That may include everything from birth control to breast cancer to hemorrhoids.

A gynecologist is clearly a woman's best choice for some of these health concerns. But even top gynecologists may lack the training or experience needed to resolve certain health problems. And as a group, gynecologists are frequently accused of abusing their patients' trust—with unnecessary surgery, half-baked psychosomatic diagnoses, and overtreatment of such natural processes of womanhood as pregnancy or menopause. For the unquestioning woman, a visit to the gynecologist can be a hazardous voyage.

Millions of women see their gynecologist each year. They go for Pap smears and breast exams, advice on contraception and prescriptions for birth control pills, treatment of vaginal infections, fertility counseling, prenatal care, and, increasingly, for osteoporosis screening, mammograms, hormone replacement therapy, and general physical exams.

Gynecologists are doctors who specialize in (and like to think they champion) women's health. They are trained to care for a woman's reproductive organs (her vagina, uterus, cervix, fallopian tubes, ovaries) and breasts (excluding the treatment of breast cancer). For about 70 percent of women, the gynecologist is the *only* doctor they see. They do not have a family doctor or internist (a doctor specializing in the nonsurgical treatment of many illnesses) overseeing their general health. For that reason, some gynecologists also act as a woman's general care doctor.

And for even more women, the gynecologist is the only doctor they see when they are *not* sick, for preventive care. For men, the nearest equivalent might be a family doctor who monitors blood pressure and cholesterol, and checks regularly for colon and prostate cancer.

At its best, gynecology does help women stay healthy, and offers them more control over their reproductive lives than ever before. But even at its best, women's health care involves risks and uncertainties that are seldom discussed in a doctor's office. And at its worst, it involves greed, ageism, sexism, paternalism, even sexual abuse.

That's why we wrote *Take This Book to the Gynecologist with You*. It's a book that will help you make the most of every visit to the gynecologist, whether you've been going for years or are contemplating your first visit.

It's a book that will help you evaluate a doctor's competency, determine whether surgery is appropriate, and find out if the drug your doctor prescribes has a record of bad reactions or if the fertility clinic you are considering has ever gotten anyone pregnant.

Most of all, it's a book about asking questions—commonsense questions that will help you get the kind of information you need to decide what's best for you, even when tough decisions have to be made. It's a book that will let your doctor know you mean business, that you don't intend to be a victim of the medical system.

—— *Choosing the Doctor*

Maybe you've gone to the same gynecologist for years for routine care, not knowing much about the doctor but feeling satisfied enough to remain his patient. (Inertia may have something to do with your choice, too.) Or maybe you see a different gynecologist every few years, not necessarily choosing carefully but hoping this newest one will turn out to be Dr. Right.

Maybe you've never seen a gynecologist, and have no idea at all what to expect. Maybe you are frightened or embarrassed by the whole prospect—or wonder whether you need to go at all. You want information that addresses your concerns from the patient's point of view, not the doctor's.

Choosing the right gynecologist for you and your needs isn't easy. There's no one place you can call for the names of good doctors, or to find out which to avoid. But the process of choosing a gynecologist is a good way to clarify what things you need to know about your doctor; what things you want or don't want in a doctor; and perhaps, some of your own weak spots as a patient. You'll weigh hard facts like a doctor's training and hospital privileges against more subjective qualities like trust and the willingness to listen and explain things.

The process of choosing a doctor does have its satisfactions. When you're done, you'll have become a better-informed medical consumer, and you'll now have as your doctor someone who's more likely to treat you as an equal partner in your health care.

So let's get started. (See Doctor Information Worksheet, page 194.)

First, you'll want to make up a list of potential doctors. Eventually, you'll narrow the list down to a few doctors with whom you'll have "get-acquainted" visits. Then, you'll make your selection.

How do you come up with names? Believe it or not, asking around is still considered one of the best ways. Ask friends, co-workers, neighbors, and relatives what gynecologist they see—and if they are satisfied. (You may be amazed by how willing women are to talk about their gynecologists.) And always ask *why* someone picked a particular gynecologist. Her answer will clue you in to whether hers was a random or reasoned choice.

If you want to find a doctor who specializes in the treatment of a particular health problem like infertility or cervical cancer, check at the library for the Directory of Medical Specialties, published by the American Board of Medical Specialists (ABMS). To locate the national headquarters of support groups

3

for people with particular medical problems, check the *Ency-clopedia of Associations* (Gale Research, Inc., Detroit, Michigan) or *The Self-Help Source Book,* 3rd Edition, 1990 (St. Clares-Riverside Medical Center, Denville, N.J.). Or call a local women's health center—they may be familiar with local doctors or self-help or support groups.

Nurses and midwives, your family doctor, chiropractor, other doctors or their wives, may know more about local practitioners and be your best sources for names of acceptable doctors.

You may also want to check the doctor referral services operated by your county medical society. While you are likely to get the names of several gynecologists in good standing in their organization (and even that doesn't mean much unless your community has a strong peer-review program) you won't get much more information. For first-hand experience or opinions, you'll need to talk with a doctor's patients or peers.

You can call a hospital with an obstetrics and gynecology department to get the names of gynecologists working there, and, possibly, their privileges at the hospital. Besides admitting privileges (which means a doctor can send his patients there) hospitals have a wide range of operating privileges, based on a doctor's abilities. One gynecologist may be "cleared" only for simple hysterectomies while another may be allowed to do extensive abdominal surgery for cancer.

Are you thinking about seeing a gynecologist who advertises in the newspaper or in the Yellow Pages of the phone book? While there's nothing wrong with advertising per se, you'll want to ask:

- Why is this doctor advertising? Obviously he wants to attract patients.
- Is he just out of medical school?
- Is he practicing in a community where a doctor-surplus creates competition?
- Is he promoting a special treatment, services, or hours?
- Has he just moved into the area (from a state where his license was revoked?)?

Your state medical licensing board will tell you if a particular doctor has a license to practice medicine in your state. If you ask, they will also tell you if the board has taken disciplinary action against that doctor. However, they usually will not tell you if malpractice charges have been filed against the doctor, or if his license has been revoked in another state. All state medical licensing boards are required by law to determine if a doctor's license was revoked in another state before issuing him one in your state. However, they are free to issue a license regardless of past history. Hospitals are required to check this information as well before offering hospital privileges, but they can choose to ignore it.

Even though more disciplinary actions are being taken against bad doctors, and the medical profession tries to present the public image that it is policing its ranks, when it comes to buying medical services, it's still up to you, and you alone, to make sure your doctor is competent.

Just as you're asking these initial questions about the doctor, you'll want to be asking yourself some questions about your personal preferences, including these questions:

■ *Do I want a doctor who is board-certified in gynecology?*

A doctor who is board-certified has taken extra training and passed the vigorous examination given by a national board of professionals in that specialty field. Board certification is an important way that doctors judge other doctors' credentials, and some will refer their patients only to board-certified doctors for a second opinion or consultation.

Gynecologists who have successfully completed a certified four-year training program in obstetrics and gynecology (called a residency training program), have practiced as a gynecologist on their own for a year or more, and have passed an extensive written and oral test given by expert gynecologists can be "board-certified" in obstetrics and gynecology by the American Board of Obstetrics and Gynecology (ABOG). It's true that this doesn't guarantee that every doctor who is board-certified is competent and ethical. And it certainly doesn't mean you need not check out the doctor other ways. But board certification *is* a good way for you to identify doctors who have earned formal recognition of skills in a specialty area.

Doctors can also be recertified in obstetrics and gynecology. Doctors who were certified in 1986 or later must take an examination to be recertified every ten years. Recertification is voluntary, though, for doctors certified before 1986. Their earlier certification remains valid for life. You may want to find out when a doctor was certified, and if he has been recertified. Recent certification or recertification means a doctor has proven to his peers that he is up-to-date on current obstetrics and gynecology procedures.

A gynecologist who is *not* board-certified can also practice, and it's possible that close to one-third of all practicing gynecologists are not board-certified. A noncertified doctor may have done his training at a small hospital that did not meet training program requirements; he may have failed his board exams (he gets three tries); he may be an "alternative" doctor who feels board certification is irrelevant to his practice. He may be just as good as a doctor who is certified. But one question you'll want to ask such a doctor is "Why aren't you board-certified?"

To find out which gynecologists in your area are board-certified, or to look up the name of a particular doctor:

Check your local library for the *Directory of Medical Specialists* published by the American Board of Medical Specialties (ABMS). This directory lists most board-certified specialists in the country by state, specialty, education, training, and membership in professional organizations of his or her specialty. Any surgeon listed is certified. (Some certified doctors elect not to be listed.) Most county medical societies and many doctors have a copy of this directory. (You can use this book to learn two other important facts about a doctor: (1) Where he did his residency training. Was it at a major university hospital? A community hospital? (2) How long he's been practicing as a doctor, based on the date he completed his residency training. Is he fresh out of school?)

You can also call the American Board of Medical Specialties' toll-free number, 1-800-776-CERT, to find out if a particular doctor is ABMS-board-certified. Or you can contact the American Board of Obstetrics and Gynecology, 4225 Roosevelt Way, N.E., Suite 305, Seattle, WA 98105. Even the Yellow Pages of your phone book may have advertisements listing the names of ABMS-certified physicians.

Do I want a gynecologist who will provide primary care?

Seven out of every ten women who see a gynecologist have no other doctor. That means their gynecologist plays the role of primary care physician. She monitors her patients' overall health and may counsel them on general health practices, nutrition, and exercise. She replaces the general practitioner, family doctor, or internist.

The primary care doctor's role is crucial. He becomes his patients' gatekeeper to the entire medical care system. He decides if, and when, a patient needs to see a specialist or to be admitted to a hospital. He makes referrals to other doctors or health care professionals like psychologists, nutritionists, and physical therapists. A good primary care doctor helps to keep a woman's health care from becoming dangerously fragmented. He keeps tabs on the interactions of different health problems and treatments, drugs, and even emotional stress.

How good are gynecologists as primary care doctors? An analysis of data from a large, nationwide study (the National Ambulatory Medical Care Survey of 1985) showed that, with the exception of cholesterol screening, obstetrician-gynecologists performed what are considered primary care services for women on a more routine basis than traditional primary care providers. During an office visit, they were much more likely than general practitioners, family physicians, or internists to do breast, pelvic, and rectal exams, cervical cancer screening, blood pressure checks, and urine testing.

Competition for women's health care dollars prompts both family doctors and internists to provide the same sort of care as a gynecologist. But the fact is that they do many fewer gynecologic procedures, even routine procedures like Pap smears and breast exams. Gynecologists claim these doctors are less likely than a specialist in the field to be up-to-date on current gynecologic practices, especially in areas of rapidly changing knowledge, like hormone replacement therapy or infertility.

Not every gynecologist is willing to act as a primary care doctor. And in some cases, a gynecologist may not be your best choice as a primary care doctor. A gynecologist has only one year of training in general medicine (and three years' training in obstetrics and gynecology). Family doctors and internists spend three or more years training to be primary care doctors. They may be familiar with a wider variety of health problems. Your best choice may simply be the doctor whose expertise you trust the most.

■ *Do I want a gynecologist who also practices as an obstetrician?*

Most gynecologists used to practice both obstetrics and gynecology. But an increasing number now limit their practice to only gynecology, or obstetrics. That's because obstetricians are the most-often sued doctors. (Eighty-five percent have been sued at least once.) As a result, their malpractice insurance premiums are the highest of any medical specialty. These premiums average about $50,000 (for $1 million coverage) with a range of $20,000 to $200,000 (in Los Angeles, where the number and cost of claims is highest in the nation). So doctors who are not willing to pay these costs have dropped their obstetrics practice. And the demand for doctors specializing in high-risk pregnancies has skyrocketed.

If a baby is in your future, you may want an obstetrician/gynecologist or possibly a separate obstetrician and gynecologist. If you're not planning to have children or are past the age of childbearing, you may prefer a doctor who practices only gynecology.

■ *Do I have a preference for seeing a male or female gynecologist?*

Do you feel strongly that only a woman doctor can have the kind of compassion, understanding, and trustworthiness you seek? Or do you believe medical training presses most doctors, male or female, into the same mold?

Although some women swear by women gynecologists, only a few facts and studies show any differences between men and women doctors.

Several studies found that women doctors see fewer patients, and have office visits that are longer by a few minutes. But it really depends on the individual practitioner.

It's also believed by some that women doctors are less likely than male doctors to be sued for malpractice. (That's something medical insurance companies are currently investigating.) If it's true, some say it's not so much because women doctors are less likely than men doctors to make errors, but because they may develop a more trusting and open relationship with their patients, which inevitably leads to fewer lawsuits.

Are women gynecologists less likely than men to reach for the knife? No one knows for sure about U.S. doctors. A study done in 1985 in Switzerland, though, showed that female gynecologists performed only half as many hysterectomies as their male counterparts. The researchers speculate that female doctors are more aware than male doctors of a hysterectomy's possible psychological impact.

"The importance of negative psychic reactions to hysterectomy is well known," they write. "Women seem to perceive this procedure as signaling a 'loss of womanhood and of attractiveness.' Female gynecologists may perhaps identify more easily with this position and be more restrictive in their indications." The researchers also speculate that the patient who seeks out a female gynecologist may be more aware of the hazards of unnecessary hysterectomies than women in general.

Whatever the case, women's demand for female gynecologists is high; a poll by Yale University researchers found that 70 percent of women would prefer to receive gynecologic care from a woman (although their primary considerations were competence, caring, and sensitivity). That demand is in the process of being filled by record numbers of women practicing and training as gynecologists. In 1978, only eight percent of members of the American College of Obstetricians and Gynecologists (ACOG) were women; in 1988 (the latest figures), 18 percent of ACOG members were women. Today, women make up half the residents in obstetrics and gynecology training programs.

You may feel less awkward or embarrassed, or believe it's

easier to talk about the intimate aspects of your life with a female rather than a male doctor. That may be true. But however important gender is to you, don't let it override competence. Don't assume that just because your doctor is a woman that she isn't going to suggest unnecessary tests or surgery or make errors, or that you don't need to question her every step of the way. You do. What's most important is finding the best gynecologist for you.

■ *Do I want a doctor who has privileges at a particular hospital?*

Privileges are rights granted to a doctor by a hospital review board that allow a doctor to admit, treat, and/or operate on his patients at a particular hospital. Privileges are given depending on a hospital's need for doctors and patients and on a doctor's qualifications. Not all doctors want privileges at a particular hospital, and not all hospitals take any doctor who comes along.

If there's only one decent hospital in town, or only one with an obstetrics and gynecology department, ask your doctor exactly what her privileges are there. Does she have admitting privileges? Attending privileges? Full or limited operating privileges? Ask even if you're currently perfectly healthy. These aren't the kinds of questions you want to be posing for the first time during an emergency situation.

If there are several hospitals, make sure the hospital at which your doctor has privileges is one that is approved by the Joint Commission on Accreditation of Health Care Organizations. (See Hospital Section for complete information on privileges.)

Now you've answered some basic questions about your preferences. The answers to those questions alone probably eliminated a number of would-be practitioners from your list. But, there are many other important questions that need to be answered. And these need to come either directly from the practitioner or someone on his staff.

To make best use of your time and money, you'll want to call the offices of the doctors still on your list and ask these additional questions before you decide to make an appointment. Explain that you are a potential new patient, and ask, first:

■ *Is the doctor accepting new patients? If so, does he have get-acquainted visits? How long are they? (Expect 10 to 15 minutes.) How much will it cost?*

If a get-acquainted visit seems odd to you, consider an even odder practice: allowing someone (even if he or she is a doctor) to examine your genitals with hardly more than a tip of the hat and a "Hello, ma'am." Anyone who's had a one-time-only visit with a rough, rude, incompetent, or perverted gynecologist will tell you it's a way to get to know a doctor all too well, and at your expense. Sitting face-to-face with a doctor, asking questions, getting answers, is absolutely essential to determine if you and the doctor you're interviewing are right for each other. And it's the only way you are going to get some essential information about that doctor before you allow him or her to examine you.

The importance of a get-acquainted visit cannot be underscored enough. A physician who will not agree to one should be given an extra amount of scrutiny. Not because he is necessarily a bad practitioner, but any practitioner who is unwilling to take the time (even if compensated) to meet and discuss his practice cannot be placed high up on the pro-consumer hit parade. This is especially true in gynecology where a great deal of variation in practice patterns is the rule. Thus, a get-acquainted visit might reveal the practitioner's views about hysterectomy, mastectomy, or any other important and controversial procedure. It is also your opportunity to sit down in a nonmedical moment and talk frankly and openly with the doctor. In essence you are interviewing one another to determine just how compatible the two of you are.

In communities with strong medical consumer awareness, get-acquainted visits are commonplace. The more they are requested, the more such visits are likely to be offered.

Let's say the doctor is accepting new patients. He does offer get-acquainted visits. You're just about ready to see him. But wait. There is still more you'll want to ask the receptionist or office manager before you spend time and money for the get-acquainted visit. The answers to these questions may be important enough to you that the wrong answer would scratch a doctor off your list.

■ *Is the doctor board-certified in obstetrics and gynecology?*

Again, this is an indication that he's had training as a specialist in this area.

■ *Does he act as a primary care physician?*

If you don't have a family doctor or general practitioner, you should know up front if you can count on this doctor to provide more than just gynecological care. Not all gynecologists are willing to do that.

■ *Does he accept phone calls from patients? At all hours? Certain hours?*

In these busy times, few things are more annoying than having to spend time and money on an appointment to see a doctor for a simple question, a referral to another doctor, to go over a routine test that shows nothing abnormal, or to ask a question about a drug you have been prescribed. These are things you should be able to talk about with your doctor, over the phone. And you shouldn't have to relay your questions, or get your answers, through a nurse or office manager if you feel you need to discuss your concerns with the doctor. If the only way you get to talk with the doctor is to pay for an office visit, you may want to consider a doctor who's more accessible by phone.

■ *Does he have evening or weekend office hours?*

If you're someone who has difficulty leaving work for a doctor's appointment, or have an unpredictable work schedule that may make it necessary to reschedule a doctor's appointment at the last moment, evening or weekend hours may be your only recourse. Besides, on top of paying the doctor's bill, who wants to lose work pay?

■ *Does he accept Medicare assignment?*

If you're on Medicare, you'll want to know up front if you are going to be expected to pay more for this doctor's services than Medicare allows plus the mandatory co-payment. Physicians who accept Medicare assignment agree to take what Medicare pays along with the required co-payment as full payment for services rendered. They also agree to do the paperwork necessary to process the claim through Medicare. Only 40 percent of America's physicians accept Medicare assignment for all procedures on all their patients. Among gynecologists, 44 percent accept assignment. Thus, it is important you ask and not assume they automatically will accept it. If they do not accept assignment you should ask yourself: Is this doctor worth that extra amount of money to me? And, by the way, even if the practitioner does not accept assignment for all his patients, he may do so for you. So negotiate this with him. Don't hesitate to negotiate since his fees and services are being negotiated by insurance companies all the time. The experience of the People's Medical Society has been that people who negotiate the issue of assignment with their practitioners usually are victorious.

■ *Does he post or publish a list of his fees?*

Doctors who make their fees for services readily accessible to their patients realize that many patients care how much their health care costs, even if they do have insurance. And for those who don't have insurance, knowing the price of a doctor's services can make the difference between having or foregoing a necessary treatment.

■ *Does he have privileges at the best hospital in town?*

Find out at which hospitals this doctor admits and treats his patients, and decide if any of those places would suit you were you to require hospitalization.

■ *Does he expect payment at the time of service, or does he have flexible payment schedules available? Does he take all insurance? Credit cards? Will he bill you?*

Again, this shows sensitivity to a person's pocketbook, and the possibility that this doctor won't send the bill collector to your house or drop you as a patient if you are going through economic hard times.

■ *How far in advance is he booked for routine appointments? How quickly can you get in?*

Some gynecologists, especially, book many of their routine pelvic exams and Pap smears a year in advance. Women needing such appointments may have to wait months. For emergency appointments, you'll want to know if the office policy is to see you the same day, within twenty-four hours, or longer.

■ *Who backs him up when he's on vacation? Is that doctor a board-certified gynecologist?*

While the doctor you choose may meet all your requirements, his back-up may be the doctor you have just left. Obviously, you cannot expect the back-up to meet all the qualifications of your first choice, but he should be someone you would be willing to accept in the case of an emergency.

With these questions answered, hopefully two or three doctors remain on your list. One may just be the one for you. The only way to find out is to meet him or her.

The Get-Acquainted Visit

Consider this a scouting-out mission. You'll want to bring along paper and pencil (or a copy of the Doctor Information Worksheet at the back of this book) to take brief notes that you can use later to compare doctors.

The get-acquainted visit starts the minute you arrive in the waiting room. Ask yourself:

- Is the waiting room crowded?
- Do people seem to wait long?
- Are you seen on time?
- Is the office staff courteous and friendly?
- Are the rooms neat and clean?

Doctors who offer get-acquainted visits are more likely to understand the concerns of medical consumers than those who expect a first-time visit to include a physical examination. These doctors realize how intrusive a physical exam can feel, especially when it's done by someone with whom you've barely exchanged words. To them, as to you, it's time well spent. You meet the doctor in his or her office, not an examining room. You get to wear clothes, not some skimpy gown. You observe each other eye to eye. You should have your questions ready to go, and pay close attention to how the doctor answers them.

- Is he addressing the heart of your questions and answering in a forthright manner? And remember—you're there for information *and* impressions. You'll want to pay attention to the doctor's overall manner and the way in which he or she regards you.
- Do you feel comfortable with this doctor?
- Is she listening to you? Interrupting?
- Can you trust her with the more intimate aspects of your life, not to mention your anatomy?

Do you want to tell this doctor if you've never been to a gynecologist before, or if this is your first-ever get-acquainted visit? (Maybe it's her first, too!) Expressing your concern and admitting your lack of experience may put you more at ease. You may be less anxious about all the things you don't know and be able to concentrate on *learning*.

Warning! Be careful, though, not to slip into a passive role, allowing an all-knowing doctor to control you and the situation. Many doctors prefer that kind of patient. They ask fewer questions, which means faster office visits and more money. You know plenty, and you certainly know *you* better than anyone else.

What if you've been going to the same doctor for years for routine care, and suddenly realize you don't know any of these important facts about him or her? Start asking questions *now*, before a serious health problem occurs. At your next visit, simply tell your doctor, "I realize there are some things I should know about you that I don't, so I want to ask you some questions." Or call the doctor's office manager. If you've been satisfied with your doctor's care, let her know that. But ask the questions anyway. If you haven't been completely satisfied with your care, use the information you get from this exchange to decide if you want to switch doctors.

Concentrate first on the doctor's background and training. Remember, you are asking simple and *legitimate* questions that any potential patient has a right to ask. You are asking questions that require only a simple, straightforward answer. The doctor should not be vague, secretive, or abrupt. Take note if you begin to feel defensive, apologetic, or intimidated. As a patient, those kinds of feelings could hamper your treatment. They could stop you from asking crucial questions or revealing embarrassing but important facts about a health problem. Don't forget. You are paying this doctor for his or her time, even during this get-acquainted visit.

You may want to ask:

■ *Are you board-certified in obstetrics and gynecology? When were you certified? Have you ever been recertified? If you are not certified, why not?*

■ *Are you board-certified in an additional subspecialty?*

These include gynecologic oncology, a cancer specialty; maternal and fetal care; and reproduction and endocrinology. And some gynecologists have a second certification in a nongynecologic specialty like family medicine.

■ *When and where did you do your residency training?*

Knowing the year your doctor completed his residency training allows you to figure out how long he has been practicing as a doctor. Some teacher/doctors say they like a physician to have at least five years of practice under his belt before they feel comfortable using him for referrals or consultation. And knowing where your doctor did his residency training, whether it's a small community hospital, a big-name medical center, or a foreign hospital, lets him know you care about those issues, that you are not taking his qualifications for granted, and that you'll be comparing his credentials with those of the other doctors you interview.

■ *Do you have additional training in any areas? (This would include gynecologic techniques such as abdominal laser surgery.) Where and when did you train? How long was your training? How many times a month do you perform this procedure?*

■ *At what hospitals do you have privileges? What hospital privileges do you have? (Full operating privileges are best.) Which of these hospitals are accredited by the Joint Commission on Accreditation of Health Care Organizations or the American Osteopathic Association?*

■ *Do you have an office operating room? What kinds of procedures do you do here? Is it certified by Medicare or by an ambulatory health care association?*

The previous questions relate to a doctor's practice, but not necessarily his or her philosophy. By asking these additional questions, you can get even more of a feel for whether this doctor:

- considers his patients as equals in their health care,
- can separate fact from opinion, and
- can explain complex and controversial issues in an understandable way.

■ *Do you share copies of medical records with your patients if they request it?*

Many doctors don't like to share medical records with patients. They think their patients won't understand what's written in them. And the records may contain comments about a patient that a doctor considers personal, and that may be insulting or embarrassing to a patient. Does your doctor think you're a LOL (Little Old Lady)? Or a crock (Crazy)?

Having in your possession copies of your medical records demystifies the process of diagnosis and treatment. It allows you to compare your recollection or your own notes of your medical condition with your doctor's records. It may help you to piece together a picture of your blood pressure, cholesterol, or some other health problem. If you need to see a different doctor, you'll know exactly what written information that doctor will receive about you. A doctor who provides his patients with easy access to their medical records isn't trying to hide anything. He isn't assuming his patients are too dense to understand the records. He isn't out to protect his "turf" at his patients' expense. He wants his patients to know what he is thinking and doing. Your doctor may charge you for copies, but he shouldn't charge more than ten or fifteen cents a page.

If you've been seeing a doctor for some time and decide you now want a copy of your medical records, simply request one. If your doctor wants to know why you want it, just say you're curious to know what's in it. Curiosity is reason enough. You don't have to justify your request.

■ *Do you give copies of test results to patients if they request it?*

As with medical records, making available copies of test results means this doctor is willing to share all information with you, and assumes you will be able to understand it, with his explanation if necessary.

■ *Are you available for occasional phone calls?*

Even if you've gotten an answer to this question earlier from the doctor's office manager or secretary, it's a good idea to also ask the doctor himself. His response will give you a feel for whether he believes it's a patient's right to talk with him by phone, or if he considers it a bothersome chore for which he is not paid.

■ *Is a female nurse in the room during the exam? Can
you bring along a female friend if you desire, or
your spouse?*

Again, honoring such requests shows a doctor is flexible
and willing to accommodate his patient's wishes. However,
some gynecologists are wary of patients who request that their
spouse be present during an exam (except, possibly, for prenatal exams). They're concerned that the husband has put
pressure on his wife to be present during the exam because
he's afraid that talk of physical or sexual abuse might arise,
or because he's so possessive of his wife that he cannot allow
her to have a pelvic exam without his presence. Gynecologists
like to avoid those kinds of husbands, and they want their
patients to be able to talk freely.

■ *Where do you send your Pap smears, and why?*

You want to find out if this doctor has picked a laboratory
based, not on its cut-rate prices, but its quality control and
accuracy. Does he know the laboratory's accuracy rate? Is the
laboratory Medicare-approved? Is it nearby or far away? (A far-
off lab may be a large discount place.) Does the lab send back
Pap smears that have an inadequate sampling of cells, or simply report the smear as negative? Does it provide a detailed
report of any abnormal findings?

■ *What percentage of your patients have
hysterectomies, and why?*

You want to get a feel for what this doctor considers necessary surgery, whether he believes a woman's uterus and ovaries are worth preserving, whether he has a certain cut-off age
at which he believes hysterectomy is the treatment of choice.

■ *At what age do you recommend women begin yearly
mammograms?*

Look for a reasoned decision, based on fact, not opinion.
Does this doctor know the issues and studies involved in current mammogram recommendations? Is he willing to discuss

them with you and let you make your own decisions, based on your personal concerns and risk factors for breast cancer?

■ *Why might you recommend hormone replacement therapy?*

Again, look for facts, not opinions. Can this doctor explain to you the controversies concerning hormone replacement therapy? Does he strongly recommend it for some conditions? Are there some women for whom he won't prescribe it? Is he open enough to allow you to make your own decision, without pressure from him?

■ *Have you ever been sued, disciplined, or had hospital privileges revoked? Where, when, and why?*

You want to see how the doctor reacts to this question. Is he matter-of-fact? Angry? A fair number of obstetrician/gynecologists have been sued, but it usually takes a number of lawsuits, or extreme negligence or unethical behavior for a doctor to be disciplined by a state licensing board or to lose hospital privileges.

Does it make a difference to you whether this doctor donates an afternoon a week of his time to a neighborhood clinic? Whether or not he performs abortions? Ask.

Is this doctor going to want to ask *you* any questions? Sure, he may, and he certainly has that right. After all, this get-acquainted visit is the first step in a possible partnership. It should not be adversarial. You ask scores of questions when shopping for a car, why not when shopping for a doctor? You should be open to questions, and answer honestly and fully. The doctor may ask: Do you have any special health problems you'd want me to treat? Have you ever had any problems with a doctor or hospital stay? If this doctor seems jumpy, he may be the type who orders unnecessary, costly, and sometimes hazardous tests just to cover all his bases. If he seems suspicious of you, it may mean he's not used to the kind of give-and-take a doctor-patient partnership involves. It may mean it's time to interview another doctor.

—— *Making Your Choice*

Use a copy of the Doctor Information Worksheet at the back of this book to make notes and compare doctors. Then, review your notes.

- Take a second look at the qualifications of the doctors you are considering; look for board certification and hospital privileges.
- Consider the type of doctor-patient relationship you could establish with each doctor on your list. Pay special attention to the doctor's attitude, professional demeanor, and attentiveness to your questions.
- Consider doctors who accept your medical insurance. Your medical insurance will protect you from high costs only if the doctor accepts it.
- Recall how well the doctor's support staff handled your first visit to the doctor. Did they seem helpful, cheery, and organized? Remember, their role is important: You may be dealing with them more often than with the doctor.

If possible, discuss your choices with the friends or family members who originally recommended the doctors. Ask them what they like most and least about the doctor.

When you finally make your choice, pick the doctor who demonstrated that he or she would be most trustworthy and capable of meeting you halfway in a good doctor-patient relationship. *That's* the doctor who's best for you.

—— *Inside Gynecology*

Selecting a gynecologist, or any doctor, is an important first step. Your choice will determine, at least in part, how you and your physician work together.

But there's more you need to know about your doctor, and gynecologists in general, to be a smart medical consumer. It is helpful to understand how gynecologists are trained, the attitudes and approaches they tend to adopt, and the different settings in which they work to help you put your medical care into further perspective.

21

Group Practice

Are you seeing a doctor who works in a group? You should ask him the same questions as you would a solo practitioner, and also get details about any other doctor in the group who might be treating you. It's important to find out if there are certain rules of the group that dictate what patients see what doctors. (That's especially important to ask in an obstetrics group. Oftentimes in obstetrics groups, the physicians like to rotate you through all the practitioners so that each one is familiar with you and your situation.) So keep the following information in mind.

These days, many doctors practice in groups. They share the same office space, staff, waiting rooms, examining rooms, and, often, patients. In 1987, 37 percent of gynecologists were practicing in groups, mostly of two or three doctors.

Group practice may offer patients the advantage of longer office hours and weekend coverage. And it may provide better medicine, at least in theory. Because it's in everyone's best interest to have a business with a good reputation, doctors practicing in groups may be more closely monitored by their colleagues than doctors practicing alone. They may keep tabs on things like how many hysterectomies each doctor in the group performs, or how many times he has complications following surgery.

One possible disadvantage: Even if you normally see only one doctor in the group, you may sometimes be expected to see another if yours is unavailable. (You can always say no, reschedule your appointment, and ask that in the future you be called before your appointment if your regular doctor is not going to be available.)

This "pinch-hit" doctor may not know you or be familiar with your health problems. He may have the chance to review only briefly your chart before seeing you, and he may never talk with your regular doctor about you. Remember, a doctor working off your chart is only as knowledgeable about you as your chart is complete. More than one hapless patient has gotten lost in this kind of shuffle. Don't let it happen to you. No matter how urgent your problem, it's a good idea to check with your regular doctor before you agree to any drugs, tests, procedures, or major changes in your treatment recommended by a different doctor.

And don't be intimidated. Simply say, "I want to talk with Dr. _____ who is more familiar with my case, before I . . . " A good physician will respect your wishes. And, before you leave the clinic, tell the receptionist you expect to either talk with the doctor by phone or to see him, without charge.

Thus, be prepared at your get-acquainted appointment with a *(continued)* physician in a group practice to ask these sorts of questions:

• Are all the doctors in the group board-certified in obstetrics and gynecology?

• Will my regularly scheduled appointments be with only one doctor, or with any of the doctors in the group?

• Will I be informed ahead of time if my regular doctor is not available for an appointment?

• How many days a week is my regular doctor out of the office? Which days are they?

And if a baby is contemplated in your future, be sure to ask:

• How likely am I to have my regular doctor during my labor and delivery?

• Do you know now if my regular doctor is planning to be out of town during the time I am due to have my baby?

• Is there a second doctor I should also be seeing in case he's the one who delivers my baby?

• What are the chances of my baby being delivered by a doctor I've never seen before?

So let's take a close, behind-the-scenes look into the making of a gynecologist. This is the inside story—things medical professionals like to keep to themselves. But they are absolutely essential for you to know if you are going to choose the best practitioner.

This information may make you skeptical, perhaps even a little angry. It will certainly confirm why, every step of the way, questions are so vital.

How Gynecologists Are Trained

What should you know about a gynecologist's training in order to make wise decisions about your medical care? Understanding the limits of a gynecologist's expertise, the things they are trained or *not* trained to do, will help you determine when it's time to see a different doctor. It will help you distinguish the tremendous differences among doctors—even those in the same specialty—in treatment recommendations, surgical skills, and the ability to communicate.

One thing to keep in mind: No doctor ever knows every-

_____

Choosing a Gynecologist in an HMO or PPO

Health Maintenance Organizations (HMOs) and Preferred Provider Organizations (PPOs) have attracted women because they provide a full line of hospital and outpatient services at a competitive rate, including routine obstetric, gynecology, and pediatric care. Traditional health insurance plans ordinarily do not cover costs of routine care provided on a fee-for-service basis.

When you join an HMO or PPO you will, in all probability, be given a list of doctors who participate in the plan. From this list you will be expected to choose a personal doctor who will provide the majority of the care you receive. In most HMOs this is a family doctor or internist, not a gynecologist. In some HMOs, women can choose to have a family doctor or internist provide routine gynecologic care, or choose both a family doctor and a gynecologist. Either of these doctors can be responsible for referring you to specialists and other health care services when appropriate.

Depending on the type of HMO you join, all the doctors may work for the HMO at one central location. You would then receive all your care, except for some outpatient surgery and hospitalization, at this HMO's site. Your choice of doctors, then, is limited by the number of doctors on staff. There is another type of HMO called an Individual Practice Asso-

ciation (IPA) which may offer more doctors. If you join this type of plan, you would see the doctor in his/her private office rather than at a centralized HMO location. In fact, your present family doctor or gynecologist may even be a part of this plan. (An IPA allows doctors in private practice to offer HMO-like coverage while still retaining their private offices. They continue to see both their private-pay patients as well as HMO patients.)

A PPO operates much the same way. Your employer gives you a list of doctors who have agreed to provide all your medical care, including hospitalization, and you are instructed that you may use any of the doctors on the list. Women may be allowed to select both a family doctor and gynecologist.

If you're on Medicare, you may want to check out a Medicare HMO, which employs doctors who accept Medicare assignment. (Your area Agency of Aging should know if one's available in your part of the country.)

Ask your company HMO-PPO representative if you can have a get-acquainted visit with some of the doctors in the plan. Some plans may permit you to interview the doctor, while others may just provide a short biographical sketch of the doctor listing medical education, board certification (if any), past hospital positions, years in practice, and years with the HMO-PPO. If get-

(continued)

acquainted visits aren't offered, make sure you inquire as to the procedure for making a change in the event that you are not pleased with the doctor you choose. Most HMOs and PPOs should have a policy on this subject, but if it isn't explained make sure you ask about it. However, be wary of any HMO, PPO, or IPA that will not allow a get-acquainted visit. It suggests they have more of a business mentality than a caring one.

Do HMOs-PPOs improve health care for women? They may in some ways, and in others, they may not. As Lynn Payer points out in her book, *How to Avoid a Hysterectomy* (New York: Pantheon Books, 1987), "Fee-for-service medicine, where doctors are paid for each service they perform, has often been cited as a cause of the high U.S. hysterectomy rate. But the spread of HMOs which do not pay doctors for each service, may not improve matters. Fee-for-service medicine provides an incentive to perform as many services as possible, and if hysterectomy is the only service the doctor knows how to perform, then he or she will have an incentive to perform hysterectomies.

"HMOs, on the other hand, provide incentives to treat the patient as inexpensively as possible. In some cases, hysterectomy is cheaper than alternatives such as myomectomy, which costs about the same but may have to be repeated. HMOs will probably help cut down on the number of hysterectomies performed when absolutely nothing is wrong with the patient, but they may make it even harder to find good alternatives when some form of treatment is necessary."

— Adapted from *How to Choose a Doctor*, a People's Medical Society Health Bulletin (see HMO Worksheet, page 195)

thing there is to know. Doctors are expected to fill in at least some of the gaps in their education as they practice medicine. They do this by reading professional journals, consulting with more experienced doctors, attending conferences and workshops, and when necessary, making referrals to other doctors. "As far as I'm concerned, the best doctor is one who knows what it is he *doesn't* know," says Robert Rebar, M.D., professor of obstetrics and gynecology at the Cleveland Clinic. "Doctors who think they know it all are the ones who get in over their heads and then make stupid mistakes."

Doctors who become board-certified gynecologists spend

Choosing a Doctor Who Accepts Medicare Assignment

Ask anyone covered by Medicare what their biggest concern is and you'll find out it's finding a doctor who will take Medicare assignment. In 1989, 44 percent of gynecologists agreed to take Medicare assignment for all their Medicare patients (compared to 40 percent of all doctors nationally). What is Medicare assignment? It's a method of paying doctors for services they provide to Medicare beneficiaries while limiting the out-of-pocket medical expenses of senior citizens. The government, through the Health Care Financing Administration (HCFA), the agency that runs Medicare, determines how much doctors should be paid for the services they provide to Medicare beneficiaries. This is known as the approved amount. Then the HCFA pays 80 percent of this amount and the patient pays the remaining 20 percent (called co-payment).

Doctors who take assignment agree to accept the amount paid by the government plus the 20 percent paid by the patient as full payment. This means the doctor would not bill for the difference between what he/she "usually" charges and what Medicare and the patient paid. For example, if Medicare allots $100 for a certain procedure, they pay 80 percent of this amount or $80. The patient pays the remaining 20 percent or $20. Even though the doctor might normally charge non-Medicare patients $150 for this procedure, the Medicare patient only pays $20, not the $70 difference.

Of course, the most direct way of finding out if your doctor accepts assignment is to ask him or her. But you have other avenues too. One place to begin looking for the names of doctors who accept assignment is the local office of the Social Security Administration. Each local office has a directory of doctors who accept Medicare assignment. It might be a good idea to call the local office ahead of time to find out when it's most convenient to look at the directory. The directory includes the names of primary care doctors as well as specialists.

You might also contact the area Agency on Aging for information on doctors who accept Medicare assignment. Very often this agency has compiled doctor directories or has worked with other community groups that have.

Another way of finding doctors who accept Medicare assignment is to join a Medicare Health Maintenance Organization. These are not available in all parts of the country, but if there is one near you it may
(continued)

deserve your consideration. But investigate first before you decide to join.

If you do join a Medicare HMO, you may or may not be required to choose a new doctor. Medicare HMOs that employ their own doctors and operate their own health cen-ters will require you to choose a new doctor. However, there are other types of Medicare HMOs that may permit you to retain your present doctor.

— from How to Choose a Doctor, a People's Medical Society Health Bulletin

four years in college as an undergraduate (majoring in everything from liberal arts to pre-med); four years in medical school (where they study subjects like anatomy, pharmacology, and chemistry); and four years in graduate medical education, called a residency training program.

It's here, in the residency program, that fledgling gynecologists get the kind of hands-on experience that molds them into doctors. In hospitals or private clinics, they learn routine gynecological and obstetrical procedures and surgery, and develop attitudes and approaches to health care that will most likely stay with them the rest of their lives. In some states, doctors can be licensed to practice medicine, including gynecology, without ever having completed a residency training program. There are no accurate statistics on how many doctors do this.

Most residency training programs are accredited by a special medical education board, the Residency Review Committee for Obstetrics and Gynecology. This committee is composed of about twelve senior doctors, both teachers and practitioners, nominated by members of the American Medical Association, the American Board of Obstetrics and Gynecology, the American College of Obstetricians and Gynecologists, and by some medical specialty societies.

Accreditation means the program curriculum meets a long list of requirements that includes things like the approximate number of hysterectomies or caesarean sections a doctor should perform before he graduates from the program. Some residency programs, though, especially those at small com-

How Many Gynecologists Are *Not* Board-Certified?

According to a report by the American Medical Association, "Physician Characteristics and Distribution in the U.S.," in 1989 there were 33,095 working gynecologists in the United States. Of them:

• 12,919, or nearly one-third, were not board-certified.

• 19,814 were certified by the American Board of Obstetrics and Gynecology.

• 118 had dual certification with the American Board of Obstetrics and Gynecology and another medical board.

• 744 were certified by a noncorresponding medical board, such as the American Board of Family Practice.

What's this mean for you? There's a 1 in about 2.5 chance that any gynecologist you see is not board-certified, which could mean the doctor has not completed a residency training program or had any training beyond the very basics of medical school. That's why it's important to ask questions about training and certification.

munity hospitals, are not accredited or have lost their accreditation because they don't offer enough training opportunities or have too few teacher/doctors on staff. Doctors-in-training who go through these programs are not permitted to apply for board certification. Again, nobody keeps statistics on how many gynecologists go through such a program.

Even among accredited residency training programs, variety flourishes. One program might specialize in high-risk pregnancy; another in invasive abdominal cancer or urinary tract surgery. Some pride themselves on their programs' low percentage of caesarean births (which means doctors learn how to handle difficult labors without resorting to surgery). Others tout their in vitro fertilization programs, which help couples conceive via modern technology.

All this variety means that, beyond the basics, some doctors will have much exposure to certain skills; others will have practically none. And none can be board-certified as specialists in cancer treatment, high-risk pregnancy, or as infertility experts unless they have completed training beyond a residency program, and passed a special test.

━━━━━ *What Gynecologists May Not Know*

━━ *Where are the "black holes" in gynecologists' education?*

- Few are well-trained in the kind of primary care that a family doctor or internist would provide. Most programs stick pretty much to women's reproductive organs. That means that although more and more gynecologists are offering care for problems like high blood pressure or obesity, they are not specially trained to treat these conditions, and probably should refer complex cases to a better-qualified doctor.

- Although communication skills (which should teach a doctor to accept a patient as an equal partner in health care) are often offered in family practice and pediatrics training programs, they have yet to catch on in obstetrics and gynecology, which is taught as a traditional surgical specialty. If gynecologists are to cultivate these skills, they have to do so on their own. Some do learn; others take the attitude "If my patients don't like me the way I am, they can leave." Most are just beginning to wake up to the fact that good communication skills result in better health care.

- Even though they are frequently the first doctor a woman sees when she discovers a lump in her breast, most gynecologists have very little training in the management of breast cancer or in mammography. (See Section 3, Breast Disease.) These two areas are currently the highly prized territory of radiologists, radiotherapists, surgeons, and medical oncologists (doctors specializing in cancer). Radiologists supervise the taking of mammograms (breast X-rays which can detect tiny lumps) and examine mammograms for signs of cancer. That's an art in itself. Radiotherapists perform post-lumpectomy radiation treatment, which needs to be done carefully to avoid damaging the lungs or creating scar tissue in the breast.

    Surgeons do breast biopsies, lumpectomies (removal of just

the lump and surrounding tissue), and all kinds of surgical removal of the breast. Medical oncologists oversee a patient's care and plan post-surgical hormone or chemotherapy regimens.

Gynecologists would like to move into this territory, although whether they could do a better job at it remains to be seen. The treatment of breast cancer is becoming increasingly complex, because, like many forms of cancer, some types of breast cancer need to be treated as systemic, or whole body, diseases. Nevertheless, some obstetrics-gynecology residency programs are setting up training in breast cancer and in benign breast disease.

- And although most gynecologists do at least some counseling in problems of sexuality, when it comes to the psychological aspects of sex, few are qualified to provide much more than a sympathetic ear. Ask any gynecologist who claims to be a sex therapist to state his qualifications. Then, check him out yourself.

  It *is* true that a gynecologist may be able to pinpoint physical problems that could be contributing to sexual problems or loss of sex drive (vaginal dryness, or low hormone levels for instance). And it's important to check out such things before you run off to a psychiatrist.

  But since sexual problems or loss of sex drive are often a symptom of more complex issues, treatment often falls to psychologists and psychiatrists, with good reason. Going to a gynecologist for what you suspect is a psychological problem is like calling a plumber when your roof leaks. You're asking the wrong person for help.

- You should know that obstetrics and gynecology is considered a *surgical* specialty. (And it's the surgical specialty that requires the least amount of actual surgical training.) It was first recognized as a distinct medical specialty around 1900, when doctors began doing caesarean sections. Specialties like family practice and internal medicine are nonsurgical specialties, emphasizing noninvasive care or drug treatment.

  Because it is a surgical specialty, every obstetrics and gynecology training program revolves around learning basic surgical procedures: caesarean sections and hysterectomies, cervical biopsies, endometrial biopsies, vacuum aspirations of the uterus, cryosurgery, colposcopy, laparoscopy, and other techniques.

While anyone who really *needs* one of these operations will be glad to know that even a fresh-out-of-school doctor has performed at least the minimum number deemed necessary to achieve competency, some women's groups feel training that emphasizes—even glamorizes—surgery is a big reason gynecologists recommend so much unnecessary surgery to women. Surgery, especially hysterectomy, is too often seen as the "definitive," or conclusive, cure, as Diana Scully points out in her book, *Men Who Control Women's Health* (Boston: Houghton Mifflin, 1980).

One reason for that attitude may be that many gynecologists still apparently feel there are no, or few, problems associated with hysterectomy, and that the problems of depression, loss of sex drive, or fatigue that many women report after this operation are overblown and of psychological, not physical, origin. "There's no proof that hysterectomy hurts anyone," says George Malkasian, M.D., president of the American College of Obstetricians and Gynecologists (ACOG) in 1989–90. Dr. Malkasian is chairman of an ACOG committee writing a position paper on hysterectomy.

- And few gynecologists learn enough about the more complicated surgical procedures that are alternatives to hysterectomy—like myomectomy (to remove fibroid tumors) or uterine resuspension (to reposition a fallen, or prolapsed, uterus)—to be skillful in doing these procedures on their own when they finally become doctors. To learn these and skills like microsurgery or laser surgery, they must take further training.

Despite their surgical training, most gynecologists go on to practices that are 90 percent preventive care. Most of their time is spent doing Pap smears, dispensing birth control information and prescriptions, treating vaginal infections, and providing routine prenatal care. It's no wonder they sometimes rail in professional journals of feeling like "triage" officers—medics whose job it is to determine the seriousness of an injury and then pass the patient on to a particular doctor for proper care.

What's Behind Board Certification

After they successfully complete residency training, gynecologists are expected to practice medicine as gynecologists for at least one year. They are then permitted to take the test offered by the American Board of Obstetrics and Gynecology (ABOG) which, if they pass, will allow them to be "board-certified." This test includes oral and written sections, and covers many areas. A doctor who fails either part of the test is permitted to re-take that part two more times over a period of ten years. If he still hasn't passed, he must go through another residency training program before he is permitted to take the test again.

Doctors who are currently working on achieving board certification are called "active candidates for the board." The vague term "board-eligible" is no longer used. Currently, about 85 percent of residency-trained gynecologists eventually become board-certified. That's a high percentage for a surgical specialty. But some 12,971, or somewhat less than half of all working gynecologists, are not board-certified, according to the American Medical Association.

Any gynecologist who was certified by the American Board of Obstetrics and Gynecology in 1986 or later is now required to take a recertification test every ten years.

Specialists

Your gynecologist may be able to take you only so far in diagnosis and treatment before she recommends that you see a specialist who has more experience in training and treatment of your condition. While it's important that your gynecologist

Is It All in Your Head? Maybe Not.

It may seem paradoxical, since over-treatment (with unnecessary surgery) is such a problem in women's medicine. But women also tend to be undertreated for real health problems because doctors dismiss their symptoms as psychological.

Studies show that doctors are more likely to write off a woman's complaints as being "all in her head" especially when an initial examination reveals nothing. In one such study, researchers examined the medical records of fifty-two men and fifty-two women who were patients in a large group practice in California. All presented with the same, non-gender-related symptoms—headache, chest pain, fatigue, or dizziness. The researchers found that, in every case, the men got a more thorough medical workup than did the women.

It's true that men do tend to have more cardiovascular disease than women, and to develop it at a younger age. But a recent survey by the Endometriosis Association found a similar tendency to slap a psychological label on pelvic pain. Many women later diagnosed with endometriosis spent years seeking help, going from doctor to doctor, being told they should have their heads examined, not their bellies.

Although it's true that many illnesses have a psychological component, and that being sick with an undiagnosed illness is distressing, don't let that stop you from getting the kind of help you deserve for a real physical problem. If a medical history, a physical examination, and a few tests reveal nothing, you may want to try talking with someone about your problems, reducing stress, exercising, and eating better. Then, if your symptoms persist, have further tests or see another doctor. What you *don't* want to do is subject yourself to dangerous and costly tests for a problem you suspect is emotional. (And sometimes, accepting that it *is* emotional is hard to do.) At the same time, you don't want to let your doctor (or a psychiatrist) designate as emotional what you truly believe is a physical problem.

knows her limitations, and it's true that seeing a specialist can be very helpful, it should not be a casual next step routinely taken in every medical situation. If your gynecologist recommends that you see a specialist, you need to find some things out:

■ *Why do I have to see a specialist?*

Or, put another way, "What exactly do you think is wrong with me?" Your gynecologist should be able to give you an understandable, point-by-point diagnostic picture. Or, if she's baffled, she should at least be able to tell you which of your symptoms are troubling enough to her that she thinks you should see a specialist. If your doctor can't or won't explain things clearly to you, or is resentful of your questions, it's possible she hasn't thought things out very well. Maybe it's time to see a different gynecologist.

■ *Why this kind of specialist?*

You need to know what's involved in this specialist's area of expertise, and what he can provide that your own doctor cannot. Knowing this will help you decide if you want to see the specialist at all. That *is* an option. Or you may decide to hold off on seeing a specialist if you're not convinced it's necessary. Let your doctor know that she must make a very good case for every step taken in your medical care.

■ *Why this particular specialist?*

Why Dr. Adams and not Dr. Smith? Is Dr. Adams the best person for the job? Is he the only doctor in town in this specialty? Are you being sent to him because he's an excellent representative of his profession, or because he and your doctor have an agreement to refer their patients to each other? While most doctors do refer their patients to other doctors they know, you want to be sure the referral is based on competency, not social connections.

Ask your doctor for the names of two or three board-certified specialists. Then check them out yourself just as you would a primary care doctor. Call the medical licensing board in your state to see if any complaints have been filed against any or all of these doctors; ask around in your community. Call each doctor's office and ask questions. The response you get may indicate to you whether this doctor cares about his patients' concerns.

Keep in mind that gynecology specialists are in big demand. Their problem is not attracting patients, but serving the large numbers who want to see them. You may need to break through a certain "Take it or leave it" attitude to get the kind of care you deserve, especially when it comes to scheduling appointments within a reasonable amount of time, seeing the doctor on time, or having her return a phone call. It never hurts to tell a doctor, or her office manager, if you feel you're getting lost in the squeeze.

Gynecology Specialists

Some gynecologists take additional two- or three-year fellowships that allow them to train with experts in certain areas of women's medicine. After they pass a test, they can be board-certified in the subspecialty of gynecologic oncology, maternal and fetal medicine, or reproductive endocrinology.

All three of these subspecialties were established in 1974. Because requirements for training fellowships limit certification, only doctors who completed their fellowship later than 1974 can be board-certified in any of these subspecialties. (Although, for a few years, practicing doctors could apply for certification in one of these subspecialties, this is no longer allowed.) This means that some older doctors who have years of experience—who may even have taught the younger specialists—have themselves never been certified. And it means that although certification is as close as you'll get to a guarantee that a doctor is qualified in her field, some doctors who *aren't* certified are just as qualified. Certification, then, while important, is no guarantee of competency, so the onus falls on you to ask questions to assure yourself of any doctor's qualifications.

Here's what each of these specialists does:

A *gynecologic oncologist* is a surgically trained doctor who specializes in the diagnosis and treatment of cancer of the female reproductive organs: the cervix, uterus, ovaries, fallopian tubes, vagina, and vulva.

Although some do have private practices, most of these doctors are affiliated with comprehensive cancer centers or teaching hospitals, and they work with a group of cancer specialists that may include radiologists, radiotherapists, pathologists, surgeons, psychologists, and specially trained nurses and technicians.

When would you see a gynecologic oncologist? It's standard care to be referred to this kind of specialist by your regular gynecologist if he suspects or has diagnosed any kind of cancer of the reproductive tract. Cancer treatment is one of the most challenging areas of medicine, with treatment regimens changing so rapidly that even experts sometimes have trouble keeping up. The odds are just too high to trust your care to anyone but an expert. If your doctor doesn't refer you, find one yourself.

You might see a gynecologic oncologist for a cervical or endometrial biopsy, for laparoscopy for suspected cancer, or for a cervical conization (especially if it's for early invasive cancer). You might consult with such a doctor for a second opinion on a pathology report (such as a cervical biopsy) or if you're concerned about a condition that has been diagnosed as a benign uterine or ovarian tumor.

And you'd definitely see this doctor if you need a hysterectomy for cancer, and for cancer that has spread beyond the uterus into the abdominal cavity. Gynecologic oncologists are the only gynecologists trained to do radical abdominal surgery for cancer. They are also experts in the use of chemotherapy and hormone treatments as cancer therapies.

One disease they *aren't* expert in is breast cancer. That condition remains the realm of surgeons and radiologists, and increasingly, medical oncologists.

Since gynecologic oncologists are in big demand, most women don't use these doctors for routine exams. (They'd probably have trouble getting an appointment, and besides, it's not necessary.) But women who've had reproductive tract cancer in the past, who have a strong family history of reproductive tract cancer (ovarian cancer, for example) or who have been exposed to DES, a hormone known to cause vaginal cancer, may see a gynecologic oncologist on a regular basis because these doctors are best trained to monitor the signs and symptoms of cancer.

Some gynecologic oncologists have a special interest in certain rare types of cancers. You may want to ask what types of cancer they treat most often. For instance, some specialize in ovarian cancer. Because there are about thirty different kinds of ovarian cancer, and correct diagnosis determines both treatment and prognosis (some are fatal within months), even such supermicrospecialists have plenty of business.

A *reproduction endocrinologist* is a doctor specializing in the treatment of infertility problems in women. (Urologists usually treat infertility in men.) This is the doctor who can diagnose and treat hormone problems; use drugs to stimulate ovulation; perform microsurgery to open blocked fallopian tubes; use a laser to blast away painful patches of endometriosis; remove fibroid tumors from your uterus in a way that restores or preserves your fertility; and make test-tube babies (a process called in vitro fertilization). These doctors are expert in the surgical techniques that minimize scar tissue formation, which is a common occurrence with any kind of abdominal surgery and which can cause pain and infertility.

When would you see such a doctor? See one if you've been trying, unsuccessfully, to become pregnant for a year or more, or for six months if you're age thirty-five or older; if your regular gynecologist has been trying to troubleshoot your infertility problem and he's reached his limit of expertise; if you've had pelvic inflammatory disease and are concerned that scarring may affect your future plans for children.

What do you need to know about these specialists? Like gynecologic oncologists, they're in big demand. Their specialty is a highly profitable one. Couples may pay many thousands of dollars for treatment with no guarantee that they'll ever produce a baby. And some doctors, and the clinics they operate, have much higher success rates than others. So you need to shop carefully. (See "Infertility," p. 131.)

A *maternal and fetal medicine specialist* is an obstetrician-gynecologist who has been trained to handle high-risk pregnancies: multiple births, mothers with gestational diabetes (diabetes during pregnancy), toxemia of pregnancy (a chemical imbalance that can result in dangerously high blood pressure), or any other kind of pregnancy problem that might endanger mother or baby.

This doctor is an expert in amniocentesis (withdrawing

fluid from the amniotic sac surrounding a fetus for analysis of birth defects), fetal monitoring (tracking the condition of the baby during pregnancy, labor, and delivery), all types of fetal surgery, the effects of drugs during pregnancy, induced labor, and the resuscitation and immediate care of premature newborns. She may also be expert in ultrasound.

Most maternal and fetal medicine specialists work in the obstetrics departments of university hospitals or large city hospitals, in groups with related specialists such as geneticists (doctors who diagnose birth defects) and neonatalogists (doctors who care for newborns). But some also have private practices.

When would you see such a specialist? Most patients are referred by their regular obstetrician-gynecologist when they are already pregnant and running into problems. Pregnant women age forty or older or women who've had previous miscarriages, stillbirths, or difficult labor and delivery might also benefit from seeing this kind of specialist—before problems occur.

Self-Designated Specialists

A doctor may belong to organizations with impressive-sounding names and display "diplomas" that look great on an office wall, but don't be fooled. They do not guarantee competency. A "college," society, foundation, and even some national or international boards often provide membership for a fee. If your doctor flashes his credentials, you may want to ask: "Is that organization sanctioned by the American Board of Medical Specialties? Does it signify that you have some kind of special training or skill?" Ask for details.

Doctors can declare themselves "self-specialists" (or say they have a special interest) in certain areas—pediatric, adolescent, or geriatric gynecology; laser surgery; microsurgery; or the treatment of certain diseases such as endometriosis or premenstrual syndrome. They cannot be board-certified specialists in any of these areas, however, because no certification category exists.

To protect yourself, you should ask the practitioner:

■ *What is your training in this area? Where, when, and for how long did you train?*

Has your doctor simply developed a personal interest in treating this condition, and been self-taught over the years? Was it part of her residency training? Did she take a weekend course sponsored by a medical equipment manufacturer? A monthlong apprenticeship with another doctor? A three-month fellowship at a university hospital? Try to get a feel for the duration and quality of her training.

■ *How many of your patients have this condition? Or, how many times have you done this procedure?*

Does she see patients every day, or several times a week, with the same condition you have? If she does, she may be more likely to be up-to-date on its treatment.

Has she been doing this procedure for years, and worked on hundreds of patients? Has she been doing it just since last week, and done three? Are you her first? Don't forget: every time a doctor learns a new procedure, someone becomes her "first-time-alone" patient. Do you want to be that patient?

■ *Do you have operating privileges at a hospital to do this procedure?*

Operating privileges mean a hospital's review committee has found your doctor's training and skills sufficient for her to safely perform this procedure in their hospital. (Some procedures are so minor, though, that they are never performed in a hospital.)

Other Health Care Professionals for Women

The medical world is full of people plying their trades. Some, such as nurse practitioners, may work with a gynecologist; others compete with them. Some might be called in to consult with your gynecologist about your health problem; others may take over for a health problem that falls outside your gynecologist's area of expertise.

Whatever the case, make sure you're in the right hands. What is this particular health care professional trained to do, and why you are being referred to her? Who will be coordinating your care? How will your doctors be communicating with one another and with you?

Health care professionals who may perform many of the same services as a gynecologist include the following:

A *nurse practitioner* must have a Registered Nurse (R.N.) degree, and many have four-year degrees in nursing. Then they take an extra year of training, often as a master's degree at a university nursing school, to learn to perform some of the basic functions of a doctor. They can train specifically in gynecologic care.

In a gynecologist's office or a women's health care clinic, a nurse practitioner may do an entire routine gynecologic exam—the breast exam, pelvic exam, and Pap smear. She can order and interpret routine lab tests, manage minor gynecologic problems such as vaginal infections, and provide care for uncomplicated pregnancies. A woman who is seeing an obstetrics and gynecology nurse practitioner might not see a gynecologist for years, and then only if she has a serious problem. In fact, experts in the medical lab business say such paraprofessionals are more likely than doctors to do an accurate Pap smear, perhaps because they take more time and consider it an important part of their job.

Nurse practitioners also play an important role in patient education, showing women how to do breast self-exams and use contraceptives such as diaphragms and birth control pills.

A *family doctor* is trained to handle most minor illnesses and injuries for men, women, and children, and to recognize a possible serious illness that requires the expertise of a specialist.

Should you take your family doctor up on an offer to provide you with routine gynecologic care? Perhaps, if it's convenient for you and your family doctor is someone you trust. Approximately 20 percent of a family doctor's practice is obstetrics and gynecological care.

You should know, though, that doctors who are certified by the American Board of Family Practice are required to take

40

only one month of gynecology and two months of obstetrics training, and that non-board-certified family doctors may have no gynecology training at all.

These are reasons that gynecologists are particularly critical of family doctors who work beyond their range of knowledge. Uninformed family practitioners are accused of prescribing wrong dosages of birth control pills or hormone replacement therapy, of giving out ill-fitting diaphragms, and occasionally of overlooking what later becomes a serious problem. That's not to say that gynecologists don't goof up, too, but they believe they're the least likely of any kind of doctor to do so when it comes to women's reproductive parts.

An *internist* specializes in the diagnosis and nonsurgical treatment of diseases, especially those of adults. While internists may set up practices in which they act as highly trained family doctors, they often subspecialize in other areas such as heart diseases, infectious diseases, arthritis, and cancer. They can be certified by the American Board of Internal Medicine.

Some people choose an internist as their primary care doctor because they believe he is better at diagnosis and is less likely than a family practitioner to need to refer them to another doctor. Internists can provide some routine gynecologic care, but they are not experts in obstetrics or gynecology. They are not required to take any training in gynecology, although they can elect to take three months' training in obstetrics and gynecology during their residency training.

Doctors who are frequently consulted on gynecologic problems include the following:

A *radiologist* specializes in the study and use of various types of radiation, including X rays, in the diagnosis of diseases. She is frequently also trained in the use of ultrasound, thermography, and other imaging equipment, such as CAT scans.

A radiologist can interpret, or "read," a screening mammogram (breast X ray) and will supervise the taking of diagnostic mammograms done when a lump is detected.

A *radiotherapist* is a medical doctor who specializes in the use of various types of radiation for the treatment of diseases. He will oversee radiation treatment to the breast after lumpectomy, and radiation treatment for some types of pelvic cancer. A related specialty, *nuclear medicine*, involves the injection of radioactive fluids into the body for diagnosis and, in some cases, treatment of diseases.

A *urologist* diagnoses and treats diseases of the urinary system. He may help to pinpoint the cause of chronic bladder infections and to diagnose and treat urinary incontinence. (Don't count on a hysterectomy to solve this problem!) Patients are usually referred by their family doctor or gynecologist when a problem is difficult to diagnose or requires surgery or treatment that only a specialist can provide. Find a urologist specializing in *women*; most treat men.

An *endocrinologist* is a specialist whose field includes the diagnosis and treatment of disorders of the endocrine glands— the pituitary, thyroid, parathyroid, thymus, the islands of Langerhans (in the pancreas), the testicles (in men), and the ovaries (in women). These doctors are sometimes involved in the treatment of obesity and diabetes. And they may be involved in the treatment of certain kinds of menstrual irregularities, diseases that include the development of masculine features in women, infertility problems that are stumping a reproductive endocrinologist, and menopause (especially severe or very early menopause).

Health care professionals who are sometimes called in for consultation on gynecologic problems include the following:

A *gastroenterologist* specializes in diagnosis and treatment of problems of the stomach and intestines—the gastrointestinal (GI) tract. Your gynecologist may send you to this doctor if she believes the source of your pelvic pain is outside your reproductive organs.

A *proctologist* is a specialist in colon and rectal surgery who deals with problems of the anus, rectum, and colon. Your gynecologist may refer you to him if you have a problem in which your rectum bulges into your vagina (rectal prolapse), for hemorrhoids, for intestinal polyps, or for pelvic pain your gynecologist suspects is related to this area of your body.

A *geriatrician* is an internist who specializes in the treatment of diseases of the elderly and the problems associated with aging. Besides looking at and treating strictly medical conditions, the geriatrician gets involved in the psychological and social well-being of the elderly patient, and in that way acts as a sort of medical social worker. These doctors are especially good at dealing with prescription drug–related symptoms in older people, physical/psychiatric problems such as Alzheimer's disease, and depression related to aging and illness. These doctors know what is and what is not a normal part of the aging process. You may want to see such a doctor if you have worrisome symptoms and your regular doctor brushes them off with "Oh, you're just getting old."

Some geriatricians (especially women doctors) may have a special interest in gynecology. But it's more likely that a gynecologist will have a special interest in treating elderly patients. It can take a special touch to calm the fear and embarrassment of an older woman who's never had a pelvic exam, for example, or to examine a woman whose vaginal thinning and dryness make insertion of a speculum painful or whose arthritis makes it impossible for her to assume a legs-up position.

A *psychiatrist* is a medical doctor involved in examining, treating, and preventing mental illness. A psychiatrist's repertoire may include everything from the noninvasive (psychoanalysis) to the pharmaceutical; her observations and diagnoses may determine that the problems may be relieved only through surgery. Because, like gynecologists, psychiatrists have been accused of abusing their power, of labeling as psychiatric problems what are really social and economic problems, if you need a diagnosis or help, choose carefully. If the psychiatrist determines that you do not need drug therapy (antidepressants, for instance), you may choose to see a psychologist instead.

A *psychologist* is a non-M.D. professional who specializes in the nondrug treatment of a wide range of emotional disorders—anxiety, panic disorders, sexual problems, work and family problems, you name it. A psychologist can work with you and your doctor in the treatment of the emotional aspects of physical disability, pain, even menopause and premenstrual syndrome. A psychologist can send you to a psychiatrist if you may need drug therapy, and then work with you and the psychiatrist.

Since these health care professionals vary tremendously in their training and treatment approaches, it's crucial to shop around, ask around, and have get-acquainted visits before you settle on one. Choosing carefully may mean a big difference in the amount of help you get.

Psychologists are required to be licensed in every state, and can be board-certified in one of eight fields of study after completing an accredited Ph.D. program and passing an examination. Only 16 percent of practicing psychologists are board-certified.

An *anesthesiologist* is a physician responsible for the safe dispensing of anesthetics, usually to patients undergoing surgical procedures. The anesthesiologist chooses the type of anesthesia to be used and monitors the patient's condition and vital signs while the anesthesia is being administered. Sometimes, especially for minor procedures done in a doctor's office or an ambulatory care center, a nurse-anesthesiologist does this work. It's important, though, that a board-certified anesthesiologist be available should a problem occur. You should *always* tell your anesthesiologist if someone in your family died suddenly and unexpectedly during an operation, or if you've ever had a close call yourself. That bit of information might save your life.

——— *When Should You First See a Gynecologist?*

The American College of Obstetricians and Gynecologists recommends that you have your first gynecologic examination by age eighteen, or earlier if

- you have menstrual problems such as abnormal bleeding or pain;
- you have a vaginal discharge; or
- you are or may soon become sexually active.

Why do they recommend a pelvic examination even if you have no problems and are not having sex? Well, it's true that they'd like you to get into the habit of seeing a gynecologist regularly for checkups, even if you don't have problems. That's part of their business. But a good gynecologist makes this first visit more than a routine exam—much more. For many young women, it's the first time outside of a health class full of giggling girls (and maybe boys, too) where you get to learn about your body, see models of it, feel where those hidden parts are, find out if you are "normal," and talk about what it means to be sexually responsible and which forms of contraception might work best for you.

"That first visit determines how a woman is going to relate to gynecologists the rest of her life," says Gita Gidwani, M.D., head of pediatric and adolescent gynecology at the Cleveland Clinic.

Scheduling this exam before leaving home to go off to college or to work means you won't end up having your first pelvic exam in a hurried emergency room or clinic, when you're in pain. (It may also mean you're less likely to end up pregnant.)

"You should be given all the time you need for this visit so that you don't have to feel scared, which is the way most women feel about seeing a gynecologist," Dr. Gidwani says. "If a woman can't relax for this exam, we postpone it until another time." That's not just because it would be uncomfortable for the woman; it's because it's difficult for a doctor to do a pelvic exam if a woman is tense. (Relaxed abdominal muscles make it easier to feel the uterus and ovaries.) Tampons, menstrual pain, and normal and abnormal vaginal discharges are all things adolescent girls want to know about.

For teenage girls age fourteen or older, the exam usually is the same as it would be for an adult. They lie on an examining table, with their legs bent and their feet raised in U-shaped "stirrup" props. A speculum, a duckbill-shaped instrument, is inserted into the vagina. For younger girls, though, the doctor can often do an exam without using stirrups and without using a speculum (or by using a small nasal speculum). "It all depends on what it is you are looking for," Dr. Gidwani says. "You don't always need to examine the cervix." Vaginal infections are not uncommon, nor are sexually transmitted diseases. Tissue growth that closes the vagina or noncancerous tumors of the ovaries are rare but possible findings.

What About Mom?

What happens when a girl comes in with her mother? It's standard practice among gynecologists to respect their patient's wishes and confidentiality, no matter what her mother wants to see or know, Dr. Gidwani says. The girl should be offered the opportunity to talk to the doctor alone, and to be examined alone or with a female nurse present. "Girls age fifteen or older almost never want their mother there," says Alvin Goldfarb, M.D., a professor of obstetrics and gynecology at Jefferson Medical College in Philadelphia. "For many, this is the first time in their lives they are being treated like adults." He and his patient agree what Mom will be told about the visit before he talks to them together. "We'll often suggest to a girl that she should talk to her mother" if she's become sexually active, he says, but moms who expect the doctor to tell all are usually disappointed.

Choosing Your First Gynecologist

You can find a doctor who specializes in pediatric and adolescent gynecology the same way you'd find any good doctor—ask around. Call the pediatrics or gynecology department at your local hospital or nearest university hospital, or call Planned Parenthood. Some four hundred doctors in the United States and Canada belong to the North American Association of Pediatric and Adolescent Gynecology (this organization does not offer referrals). Members are not necessarily experts, but they do have an interest in this area. You'll want to ask them the same sorts of questions you'd ask any doctor:

- Are you board-certified in gynecology or pediatrics?
- Have you done a fellowship in adolescent and pediatric gynecology?

- Are you affiliated with a university or teaching hospital?
- What percentage of your patients are teenagers or younger?
- For what kinds of problems do you see these patients?
- Can a female friend, older sister, or mother be present during the exam if the patient requests it?

Clinics like some operated by Planned Parenthood, listed in most phone books, are the first stop for many sexually active teenagers. They provide gynecological exams, birth control and abortion information, AIDS testing, and treatment for sexually transmitted diseases to anyone, any age, with complete confidentiality, pay-what-you-can or free.

——— *Am I Ready?*

So far we have covered a lot of ground. But like all worthwhile trips, a great deal of preparation is necessary. What we have looked at so far are the people; next we must look at the accommodations.

In the next chapter we tour the places where gynecologists do their work. As you will see, knowing deluxe from run-of-the-house, and when each is appropriate, will only enhance your journey through medical-land.

___

CHAPTER TWO

The Gynecological Settings:

Inpatient/Outpatient Services

Many gynecologic surgical procedures once done only in a hospital operating room are now done on a same-day, outpatient basis. Endometrial and breast biopsies, tubal sterilization, and laparoscopies are all routinely performed on an outpatient basis. Even abdominal laser surgery and vaginal hysterectomies are sometimes done as walk-in/walk-out procedures. Medical techniques that allow abdominal operations with only a small incision or permit surgery inside the uterus through the cervix mean less blood loss, fewer infections, and a shorter recovery time for most women. Nevertheless, these are serious procedures and they do have risks. (See "Outpatient Settings," p. 52, for more information on outpatient procedures.)

Outpatient surgery definitely saves you time. You sidestep the lengthy process of being admitted to the hospital, spend less idle time prior to surgery, have fewer dubious medical tests, and get to go home the same night and sleep in your own bed.

And because you're not paying hospital overhead, or for a night's stay, your costs can be cut by as much as half. That's one reason so many insurance carriers now prefer many procedures to be done on an outpatient basis, and why Medicare has approved outpatient performance of more than twenty-eight hundred medical procedures.

If you have full medical insurance coverage, you may not

think too much about costs. But the fact is that we all eventually help pay America's astronomical medical bills, in one way or another. And if you don't have health insurance, or are having a procedure your insurance won't cover, same-day outpatient surgery is all the wiser.

Inpatient/Outpatient Services: When Should You Use Them?

Once you decide to go ahead with a certain test, procedure, or surgery, chances are your doctor isn't going to ask you where you want it done. He'll tell you. He'll have decided whether you will be an inpatient with an overnight stay in a hospital, or an outpatient at an ambulatory surgical center or the doctor's office itself.

You may ultimately agree with your doctor's choice, but you should ask some questions first to determine how he made his selection. Doctors base such decisions on two factors: (1) where insurance companies and Medicare have deemed the procedure can be done safely and at lowest cost, and (2) whether you have any health problems that would require you to be hospitalized, regardless of whether your procedure is normally done as an outpatient. In such cases, insurance companies may or may not agree with a doctor's decision. So it's essential to check with your insurance company first to make sure they will pay for your procedure when it's done in an uncustomary setting.

"Physicians are under enormous pressure at the moment by third-party reimbursers who are trying to stop patients from coming into hospitals," says Wulf Utian, M.D., director of obstetrics and gynecology at the University Hospitals of Cleveland and chairman of the department of reproductive biology at Case Western Reserve University in Cleveland. "So if I have a seventy-five-year-old woman with heart disease and I want her in the hospital the day before surgery to get stabilized and tested, the insurance company may say they won't pay for that night. They want her to come in at seven o'clock that morning, one hour before surgery. I may think it's a medically incorrect decision, but the insurance company is not likely to back me up on that."

In such cases, it's possible for a patient to petition her insurance company. "We tell our patients to do that all the time," Dr. Utian says. "But the insurers seldom change their minds." A patient can also opt to pay the extra charges herself.

Insurers do pay if an outpatient develops a medical problem that necessitates she be moved into a hospital. "They don't argue about that at all," Dr. Utian says.

So ask your doctor:

■ *Is this procedure normally done on an outpatient (or inpatient) basis?*

You want to find out if your doctor has selected the normal, customary setting for this procedure. (If in doubt, call Medicare or your insurance company.) If your doctor hasn't chosen the customary setting, ask:

■ *Why have you chosen this setting for me?*

Your doctor may list high blood pressure, diabetes, pregnancy, extreme overweight, or other health problems that she feels add enough risks to your surgery that you should be hospitalized.

■ *What other settings might be appropriate?*

Ideally, you'd like to hear "None. This is the best place for you." If you hear "Well, I'd like to put you in the hospital, but your insurance company probably won't pay for it," you may want to call your insurance company yourself. Or perhaps you'll settle on a hospital outpatient clinic, where, if you run into problems, you can be admitted to the hospital overnight.

Are you worried that you should be in a hospital when your doctor has said it's not necessary? If so, voice your concerns. If you're very frightened and think you may want general anesthesia, rather than the local your doctor is recommending, tell her. You may be able to have general anesthesia for your procedure and still be an outpatient. (Do know, though, that general anesthesia has its own risks.) If you're worried about fending for yourself when you return home, ask your doctor about lining up a day or two of in-home nursing care. Then call your insurance company to find out what's required to have this service reimbursed. (For more information on the differences between inpatient and outpatient services, see p. 48.)

Many gynecological procedures that only a few years ago were done in a hospital are now regularly done on an outpatient basis. Optical scope instruments, lasers, and improved surgical techniques mean fewer open-abdomen operations, less bleeding, and faster recovery times.

Minor procedures such as cervical biopsy, aspiration endometrial biopsy, and needle aspiration of breast cysts are done in a doctor's office.

The following gynecological or breast surgery procedures are approved by the Health Care Financing Administration, which oversees the Medicare program, for outpatient surgery at an ambulatory care center:

- Incision and drainage of perineal abscesses (in the tissue between the anus and vagina)
- Incisions of the vulva and vaginal opening
- Marsupialization of Bartholin's gland cyst (creating a pouch where once was an enclosed cyst in these small mucus-producing glands in the vagina)
- Excision of a Bartholin's gland
- Destruction of vulvar lesions of any size, by any method
- Culdocentesis (puncture of the abdominal cavity through the blind pouch behind the cervix, at the back of the vagina, to withdraw fluid near the ovaries to check for blood; might be done in the case of suspected ectopic pregnancy or ovarian cyst)
- Extensive biopsy of vaginal tissues, requiring sutures
- Excision of vaginal septum (extraneous tissue)
- Repair of enterocele, vaginal approach (repairing, through the vagina, intestine that is bulging into the vagina)
- Dilation of vagina under anesthesia (this procedure might be done if surgery or radiation treatment has scarred and constricted the vagina)
- Pelvic examination under anethesia (this procedure is done during the sometimes painful pelvic examination to determine

the spread of cancer, for people with cerebral palsy, children, and retarded adults)

- Culdoscopy, diagnostic (insertion of a viewing scope through an incision at the back of the vagina into the abdomen, which allows a view of the back of the uterus and ovaries)
- Cone biopsy of the cervix, with or without dilation and curettage
- Plastic surgery repairs of the cervix
- Dilation and curettage
- Biopsy of one or both ovaries
- Laparoscopy of the pelvic organs for diagnosis or for multiple biopsies; aspiration of cysts; destruction of adhesions; destruction by cautery or laser of lesions
- Mastotomy (incising the breast) with exploration or drainage of abscesses
- Excision of breast cysts, benign or malignant tumors, or duct or nipple lesions
- Mastectomy, partial, complete, or subcutaneous

Procedures not on this list, such as abdominal and vaginal hysterectomies, are usually done in a hospital.

——— Outpatient Settings

Ambulatory surgery is done in three kinds of settings: doctors' offices; freestanding surgery centers (away from a doctor's office or hospital); and hospital outpatient facilities (where most outpatient surgery is done these days). Costs are usually highest at hospital outpatient clinics, followed by freestanding clinics and then doctors' offices. Your doctor will suggest one of these three places, based on the extent of your surgery, your medical condition, the capabilities of her own office facilities, and where she has permission to operate ("operating privileges").

What do you need to know to have outpatient surgery done safely? You'll want to ask these questions about the facility where the surgery is being performed, whether it's in the doctor's own office or in a hospital-affiliated clinic:

■ *Can you see beforehand the place where your surgery will be done?*

Look for general overall cleanliness as well as professional ambiance. Check the recovery room, too, to make sure you will have enough room and privacy.

■ *Is the center licensed by your state health department?*

Call your state health department to find out, and while you're at it, ask if any complaints have been lodged against the facility or its operators. Licensing means a facility meets certain minimum requirements set by state law. These requirements deal mostly with the safety and cleanliness of the center's building and work areas, not with the qualifications of its employees. Not all states require licensing, but in states that do, an unlicensed facility should be avoided.

■ *Is the facility certified by Medicare/Medicaid?*

You can call the clinic's business manager to find out. Medicare/Medicaid certification is a valuable plus in the center's favor. It means that the site has been inspected and that both the facility and staff meet certain criteria related to safety, cleanliness, and emergency procedures.

■ *Is the center accredited by the Accreditation Association for Ambulatory Health Care or the Joint Commission on the Accreditation of Health Care Organizations?*

Accreditation is meant to set and promote high levels of quality, and to reward those institutions that achieve these levels. It can help the medical consumer avoid the subpar, although licensed, facility. Accreditation means that a center and its staff are reviewed on a regular basis to make sure the facility meets certain standards and offers good-quality care. Even if the center you'll be using is accredited, don't neglect to ask questions about the site and staff and to look around the place yourself.

Contact these two organizations to see if the ambulatory care center you plan to use is accredited:

Accreditation Association for Ambulatory Health Care
  9933 Lawler Avenue
  Skokie, Illinois 60077
  1-312-676-9610

Joint Commission on the Accreditation of Health Care
  Organizations
  875 North Michigan Avenue
  Chicago, Illinois 60611
  1-312-642-6061

■ *What volume of surgery does the center perform in a year?*

Many studies now show that practice makes perfect when it comes to surgery. One report's estimate of the optimum number of surgeries per year for outpatient clinics is 1,200 to 1,500 (*Consumer's Digest*, January/February 1987).

■ *What kind of nursing staff runs the center?*

Nurses play a crucial role in ambulatory surgery, even more so than in a hospital. They prepare you for surgery, assist during the operation, monitor your vital signs, and provide virtually all your care in the recovery room. Ask questions to determine if the nurses who will be working with your doctor are fully trained and familiar with the procedure:

- How often do they assist with this procedure?
- Are they full-time employees of the center?
- Are they registered nurses (RNs)? Licensed practical nurses (LPNs)? Nurse practitioners?

LPNs have the least amount of nursing school training, although they may have years of experience. Nurse practitioners have extra training in areas such as anesthesia, gynecology, and childbirth.

■ *What life-support equipment is available on-site?*

A cardiac defibrillator to jump-start a stopped heart? A properly supplied "crash cart" equipped with emergency first aid items such as endotracheal tubes and cardiac medications? Is the staff trained in life-support techniques, especially cardiopulmonary resuscitation? And if there is an emergency, to what hospital will you be transferred?

■ *What happens if you do not recover completely enough to be sent home safely that day?*

This is especially important if you are using a freestanding facility with no hospital affiliation. Are there provisions for hospitalization, or are you on your own? Will they call an ambulance for you, or will you have to make any necessary arrangements yourself?

■ *Will your insurance cover this surgical procedure when it's done on an outpatient basis?*

Some insurance policies provide coverage for hospital outpatient centers but not for freestanding surgical centers (or only for those that are accredited). And some health insurance policies require that you check with the insurance company before your surgery is done. Your insurance company may require a second opinion, to make sure your surgery is necessary. If you fail to check with your insurance company before your surgery, you may find that you have no coverage or have reduced coverage.

■ *What clothes should you wear or bring with you?*

If you are having an abdominal procedure such as laparoscopy, your belly will probably be swollen and sore afterward, so a dress or loss-fitting pants will be most comfortable.

■ *What postsurgical provisions do you need to make?*

The surgical center may insist that you be driven home after your surgery, and this is wise advice to take since you've been so recently sedated. If you're single, you may want to ask a friend to stay over your first night home. Your friend may not have the kind of nursing skills you'd get in a hospital, but he or she is probably just as good at giving a backrub, getting glass of water, or leading you to the bathroom in the middle of the night.

■ *Is your doctor going to be doing the surgery?*

If so, make sure he's qualified to be doing it. Does he have operating privileges to do this same procedure in the hospital? (If he doesn't, ask why. It may be that the procedure is so minor that it's never done in a hospital. Or it may mean that no hospital considers your doctor skilled enough to perform the procedure.) Ask:

- How many of these procedures do you perform in a year?
- What kinds of complications have you had?
- Have you ever had to do an emergency transfer to the hospital while doing this procedure? Why? What happened?

Although there's no proof that doctors who work alone and who operate in their offices are more prone to mistakes (or sued more often for malpractice), many insurers and even doctors say that physicians are more likely to be scrutinized by their peers if they work in groups, use freestanding medical facilities (which grant operating privileges just as do hospitals), or use hospital outpatient clinics.

■ *Does your doctor intend to simply diagnose your problem, or will she also correct it during the same procedure?*

If your doctor is going to be doing a diagnostic procedure such as laparoscopy (inserting a scope through an incision into your abdomen) or hysteroscopy (inserting a scope through your cervix into your uterus), find out what she intends to do if she finds something that needs to be treated. (She may be looking for abdominal scar tissue, endometriosis implants, uterine polyps, or fibroids.)

If she says she won't do anything, that she will simply schedule you for surgery at a later date, you may want to ask what would be required for you to have the surgery during the initial diagnostic procedure. It may mean, simply, that you'll have to have the procedure done in a different place. Some doctors don't have an in-office operating room sophisticated enough for them to do surgery; but they will do one-step diagnosis and surgery in a surgical center or hospital outpatient clinic.

■ *If your own doctor is not doing the procedure or surgery, what doctor is? And when will you get to meet him?*

You and your doctor should discuss his choice for your surgery. Why this doctor? What other doctors might he also recommend? Is the doctor he's recommending board-certified in gynecology? At what hospitals does he have privileges? Is he the best doctor in town to do this procedure? The only doctor in town who can do it?

Make sure your doctor knows that you expect to have an office visit with this doctor well before your surgery or procedure, and that you will be asking this doctor questions to assure yourself that he is qualified. You don't want to meet your surgeon minutes before your operation. Ask this doctor the same questions you'd ask any doctor prior to a procedure or surgery:

- Do you have operating privileges to do this same procedure in a hospital?
- How many of these procedures do you perform in a year?
- What kinds of complications have you had?
- Have you ever had to do an emergency transfer to the hospital while doing this procedure? Why? What happened?

Overnighter

If you're having major surgery or a particularly risky test or procedure, if you're pregnant, or if you're very old or in precarious health, your doctor may want your work to be performed in a hospital operating room. This means that you'll be admitted to a hospital for at least one day and night, perhaps for several, which might suit you just fine if your idea of a vacation includes plenty of "horizontal" time, in bed.

It also means that you and your doctor will have to select the hospital you'll be using. (You *don't* want to be automatically sent to the one that's most convenient for him, unless it's also the best choice for you.)

And it means that you will be exposed to additional risks simply because you will become a hospital patient for a few days.

What do you need to know about hospitals to pick the one that's best for you? For starters, you need to know at which hospitals your doctor has what are called "privileges." (Ideally, this is information you should get well in advance of any need for hospitalization, perhaps during a get-acquainted visit.)

Privileges are rights or advantages granted to a doctor by a hospital review board that consists of administrators and other doctors working at the hospital. This board looks at a doctor's training and experience and decides whether or not to give her privileges at their hospital. These privileges include

- Admitting privileges only—Your doctor can admit you to this hospital, but another doctor must care for you while you're in the hospital.
- Attending privileges—Your doctor both admits you and takes care of you, but does not perform surgery on you.
- Operating privileges—Your doctor is deemed qualified to perform surgery in this hospital. Many hospitals give doctors restricted operating privileges. They allow them to do some operations but not others. Full operating privileges means a doctor can do any kind of surgery she wants in this hospital.

Not all doctors want privileges at all hospitals. On the other hand, most hospitals do not dispense privileges to just anybody with a medical school diploma. It's a game of give-and-take. A physician needs a place to send sick patients, and a hospital needs sick patients to fill beds.

Since 1965, hospitals have been considered legally responsible for doctors' actions within the hospital. That's one reason hospitals have review boards to check a doctor's qualifications and performance and to give or revoke privileges. But hospitals are also hungry for patients, and sometimes doctors doing the most surgery—necessary or not—are kept on because they bring in good money. They may be excellent surgeons (studies show that for surgeons, practice makes perfect), but before you give the go-ahead for such a doctor to operate on you, you want her recommendation for surgery to be backed up by conservative, independent second and third opinions.

Some rural hospitals, desperate for doctors, may have less restrictive privileges than do hospitals in urban areas. So even if your doctor has operating privileges, it's important to ask questions to make sure she does your sort of operation frequently and is well skilled in the procedure.

If you live in a community that has several hospitals, your doctor may have privileges at more than one, perhaps all of them. What you want to know is: How does he go about selecting a hospital for you? Ideally, his choice should be that one of his privilege hospitals best suited to handle your condition. If his choice seems odd—you're to check into a small general hospital for major gynecologic surgery instead of the big university hospital just down the street—it could be that the appropriate hospital has refused affiliation to your doctor for one reason or another. Check on that.

If a hospital in your area has a large, well-known obstetrics and gynecology department, you'll want to know what kinds of privileges, if any, your gynecologist has there—the more, the better (full operating privileges are tops). If your doctor has no privileges, find out why. It may be that the review board of this hospital considers your doctor more of a liability than an asset to the hospital. Even if your doctor says he has never applied for privileges at such a hospital, ask why. Is he hiding something?

Is there a large medical center or university-affiliated teaching hospital in your region? Privileges at such hospitals are considered a sign of prestige among professionals. Especially if such a hospital has a certified residency training program in obstetrics and gynecology, you'll want to know if your doctor has privileges there. If he does, it means he works and operates in an arena that is regularly scrutinized by doctors who are experts in the field. If he doesn't, ask him why. Not all doctors want to pursue the "big time." And not all are granted access.

Some doctors choose hospitals for their patients based on factors other than the patient's needs. Your doctor might put you in a hospital where he currently has other patients; this makes it quick and easy for him to see all his patients without having to drive among hospitals. Such a choice, if made pri-

59

marily for his convenience, might compromise the quality of your care.

Or your doctor might have a quota arrangement with a hospital that requires him to admit a certain number of patients to that hospital each year or else lose his privileges. Again, if the hospital seems an odd choice, ask why it's being selected.

Specialty Hospital or General Hospital?

The two major categories of hospitals in the United States are specialty hospitals and general medicine/surgical hospitals.

A specialty hospital takes care of only one kind of medical condition or one type of patient. It might admit only patients with cancer or with eye problems, or only women or children, for example.

Since these hospitals concentrate on a single disease or type of patient, day in and day out, presumably the staff becomes expert in dealing with it. Many will argue that there is no better place to go than to a hospital that specializes in your particular condition. And indeed, studies do show that hospitals get better at a procedure they perform often, and the results are usually better, too. You don't want to agree to unnecessary surgery, but once you know for sure your surgery is required, your best bet is a hospital that handles many of your type of case, and a surgeon who does plenty of your type of operation.

There are some minuses to specialty hospitals, though. One drawback in some otherwise excellent specialty hospitals is limited emergency facilities. If you are in a hospital specializing in the delivery of babies and you suffer a heart attack, for example, the hospital may be able to do nothing more than stabilize you, then transfer you to another hospital to take care of this unexpected development. General medical and surgical hospitals are equipped to handle a larger variety of medical problems, including emergencies. These facilities are what most people picture when they hear the word *hospital*. They are, in effect, a collection of little specialty hospitals under one roof. (Some even have separate hospital or clinic names.) Still, a general hospital sometimes sends a patient to a specialty hospital for more knowledgeable care.

Community Hospital or Medical Center?

Community hospitals like to present the image that they are warm, friendly places, a part of the neighborhood just like the local college or theater. Such hospitals may have as few as fifty beds or as many as several hundred. A good-size community hospital has about 250 beds and provides most of the kinds of services, technology, and departments you'd expect at a hospital. Their big selling point? They are large and sophisticated enough to give you big-time medicine, yet small enough to provide that personal touch. Basic obstetrics and gynecologic services are standard offerings at most community hospitals. This is because these services are in demand and are highly profitable for hospitals.

The advantage of medical centers, on the other hand, is that they are big institutions serving a large region, and therefore they treat a wide variety of kinds of people and illnesses. They are able to diagnose and treat rare conditions that might leave community hospital doctors scratching their heads in puzzlement. These medical centers are usually affiliated with a university. This is considered a plus among medical professionals because it implies that all the newest medical ideas, machines, techniques, and drugs are available for use here. It also means that it attracts doctors who are experts in their fields, who may teach, work, and do research at these hospitals. When it comes to rare gynecologic cancers, unusual sexually transmitted diseases, or high-risk pregnancies, count on the large medical centers to provide the best care.

But that's only part of the deal. It's true that a big hospital provides doctors with lots of patients to see, work on, and learn from. For a patient hoping for a relaxed and quiet recuperation or personalized care, however, a medical center or other large hospital is probably not the place.

And if you are suffering from too mundane an illness, say, common fibroid tumors, don't necessarily expect to see or be treated by the world-famous doctors said to be lurking in the halls of your medical center. Chances are they won't be interested in your illness unless it's extreme or unusual or unless you're lucky enough to have the disease-of-the-week. You may be treated by their disciples, doctors-in-training who will give you more than enough attention, but without the glamour of a medical superstar.

Obviously, a hospital's size is not the only way to judge its character. You may get warm, caring treatment at a monster-sized hospital. (Some major cancer centers have better staff-to-patient ratios than many community hospitals.) And you may be treated like yesterday's oatmeal at a small community hospital. You need more information if you are to make a wise choice. You want to protect yourself from costly mistakes, in terms of your wallet *and* your health. Feeling angry because you're being neglected can take your energy away from getting better.

Teaching or Nonteaching Hospital?

The reasons for going to a teaching hospital are pretty much the same as those for going to a medical center: you'll get expertise, the newest technology, and the very latest medical know-how. In fact, many of the best teaching hospitals are university medical centers. These hospitals are on the cutting edge when it comes to obstetrics and gynecologic research and the development of new, and better, surgical techniques. Their staffs include nationally known doctors who are experts in even the most obscure gynecologic problems.

One possible drawback, though, is that these hospitals exist as much for the education of medical students as they do for the care of patients. Be prepared to be used as a living anatomy lesson if you become a patient at a teaching hospital. (And be especially wary if you are in for a below-the-belt problem. How many eager young doctors can you tolerate peering into your vagina or poking your ovaries? Of course, you can say "no" to any examination, and your doctor should always ask your permission before allowing students to view or participate in your treatment.)

Do all the care and attention a patient receives in teaching hospitals add up to a superior experience? A major University of Chicago study showed greater patient dissatisfaction with teaching hospitals than with nonteaching hospitals. This seemed to surprise researchers, who note that "because higher-quality care is associated with teaching hospitals, and because patients are referred to teaching hospitals for care unavailable in nonteaching institutions, it was assumed . . . that the data would show patients more satisfied with the quality of care in teaching than nonteaching hospitals." Yet this was not the case.

What will it be for you—a teaching or a nonteaching hospital? Your condition, your personality, and your pocketbook (teaching hospitals can cost up to twice as much as nonteaching hospitals) will all help determine your choice. And even more so will your need for uncommon sophistication among your care-givers. Weigh your options carefully, given what you now know.

Profit Versus Nonprofit?

All hospitals like to present a certain old-fashioned, altruistic image—that they are there to *serve* you, the patient, and your community, and that no one in need gets turned away from their doors. In truth, though, the picture is much different. All hospitals today have to keep their bottom line in mind. Even nonprofit hospitals have to meet their expenses (even if it's through charitable donations) to stay in business. And for-profit hospitals exist strictly to make money.

Does it matter to you if you go to a nonprofit or a for-profit hospital? In terms of your care, it might not. But philosophically or financially, it might make a difference. Hospitals are owned by religious orders, universities, governments (federal, state, county, or municipal), doctors or groups of doctors, health maintenance organizations and other kinds of health plans, and, increasingly, national chain corporations, which own and manage hospitals in regions or across the country and whose stockholders reap their profits.

Some hospitals, usually public hospitals in big cities, provide more charity care than others. If you are concerned about

63

being able to pay your bill, call up the hospital and ask: "How do you handle people who can't pay their hospital bill?"

You should know that for-profit hospitals may cost you more, because of markups on some services and items and because these hospitals tend to do more tests.

Before your doctor makes arrangements for you to attend a certain hospital, find out who owns it and how that ownership might affect your care and its cost. Whether your concerns are political, personal, or financial, you should know the setup before you become a patient.

―――― *Special Considerations*

What do you need to know about the gynecological care at the hospitals you have to choose from in order to make a wise choice, or to determine that your doctor has made the best choice for you?

■ *How much business does the hospital do in obstetrics and gynecology?*

Find out how many gynecologic procedures, both major and minor, were performed at the hospital during the previous year, and how many babies were delivered. If your doctor can't provide this information, call the hospital's administration office, or the office of the chief of the obstetrics and gynecology department. This is the kind of information professional evaluators use to determine whether a hospital has an active, viable, and up-to-date obstetrics and gynecology department, says Norman Gant, M.D., director of the American Board of Medical Specialties division of maternal and fetal care.

Although it's difficult to say exactly how many procedures and deliveries a hospital should be doing to stay current (and the number done varies depending on the size of the town in which the hospital is located), this information can help you choose among the hospitals you are considering, Dr. Gant says. (The higher the numbers, the better.) "A hospital's got to have a certain volume so that the nurses and hospital laboratory, as well as the doctors, are competent," Dr. Gant says. "I'm not knocking a single, isolated doctor in a rural community for performing a real service, but if you are near a metropolitan area with moderate-size hospitals, it would be reasonable to expect that a hospital would be doing about fifteen hundred deliveries a year. That would indicate it has an active ob-gyn [obstetrics-gynecologic] department."

Here are other questions you should ask:

■ *How many times a year (month, week) is the type of surgery I'm having done at this hospital?*

Try to get a feel for whether your surgery is commonly, occasionally, or rarely done; whether it's done more or less often at this hospital than at the other hospitals in town; or whether it's so seldom done at any of the hospitals you are considering that you'd be wise to make a trip into the nearest city to have it done.

■ *How many hospital beds are devoted just to gynecological surgery?*

This will help you to distinguish between a hospital's obstetrics service and gynecology service, which are usually on separate floors.

■ *Are all your ob-gyn staff doctors board-certified or active candidates for board certification in obstetrics and gynecology?*

This assures that the doctors have gone through additional training after medical school. If they are not all certified, what percentage of them are certified?

■ *Do you have doctors who are certified in gynecologic oncology, reproductive endocrinology, and maternal and fetal care?*

Having these superspecialists working in a hospital's ob-gyn department is a sign of its quality. And who knows? You may need one of these doctors for consultation during your hospital stay.

■ *Do you have a board-certified residency training program in obstetrics and gynecology?*

This indicates that this department qualifies as a place where new doctors can be trained. It means that doctors who work there are expected to stay up-to-date on research and treatment approaches, and that they are more likely to be scrutinized by their colleagues than are those at a hospital without such a program.

Do you need or want to go to a hospital that specializes in the care of women? This question is best answered only after considering the larger issue of what kind of hospital can provide you with the best possible care.

You should know that very few such hospitals exist these days: most of the older "women's" or "lying-in" hospitals have been incorporated as departments or hospitals-within-hospitals of larger institutions. There's a good reason for this: it makes a wider variety of services, including emergency medical care and cancer specialists, available to patients.

Large, well-known obstetrics and gynecology departments do have advantages: they are likely to offer the most up-to-date treatment options, because they employ doctors who are experts, teachers, and researchers in their field; they probably have the latest medical equipment, and staff who know how to use it properly; and because they do a large volume of gynecologic work, their nurses, hospital laboratory, pathologists, and others are all trained in this area. Some ob-gyn departments may also have more women (especially doctors) on staff; better postoperative educational services than smaller hospitals; and more social workers, counselors, and support groups.

You probably are not going to want or need to go to such a hospital if you determine that your local hospital can provide the care you need. But you should talk with your doctor about going to a special hospital if you require a procedure or operation that is not often done at your local hospital; if the procedure or surgery is complicated or risky; if you might benefit from medical equipment that's not available at your local hospital; or if you or your doctor want ongoing advice from a doctor who's an expert on your condition.

You might also bypass your local hospital for one that specializes in women, or that has a large gynecology department, if

- You are diagnosed with cancer of the reproductive tract and need to see a gynecologic oncologist, especially if you are seeing one who specializes in certain types of gynecologic cancer, such as ovarian cancer.
- You are fairly young (say, age fifty or younger) when you are diagnosed with cancer, or if you are diagnosed with a fast-growing cancer or your cancer is found at a later stage.
- If you need chemotherapy, hormone therapy, or radiation treatments after surgery for cancer.

Why? Because these health problems are life-threatening, and treatment for them changes so quickly that even the experts sometimes have trouble keeping up. Such conditions often require the expertise of doctors who see and treat them on a regular basis. This is most likely to be available at a large women's hospital or at a gynecology department within a large hospital.

——— Making Your Choice

Before you say "yes" to your doctor's choice of hospitals, consider your needs and options. In fact, it's wise to find out about all the other hospitals he *could* be sending you to before you agree to the one he's picked. Ask him to describe each of the hospitals at which he has privileges. If he has privileges at only one, and that hospital is not to your liking, discuss this with your doctor and try to come up with an alternative. Or look for a doctor of comparable ability with admitting privileges at that hospital. All your efforts—your questions, demands, and scrutinizing—will pay off in the end.

What you want to hear from your doctor is *not* "I send all my patients to that hospital," or even "Because it's the best hospital in town." You want to hear "Because it's the best hospital for *you*." And then you want to know *why*. Get specifics. Does it have superior recovery rates? The kind of special medical equipment you may need? Best nursing care? If your doctor seems exasperated with your tenacity, maybe it's because he's never asked himself these questions, much less been asked by a patient. Consider it an education for both of you, and ask and keep asking until you get satisfactory answers.

If the best hospital in town for your condition is booked up, your doctor may try to admit you to his second choice, if he has privileges there. Unless your surgery is urgent, tell your doctor you'll wait until he can get a bed for you in the best hospital.

Feeling confident about your medical care is an important part of the healing process, so, if you can avoid it, don't check into a hospital believing it's "second best."

Dangers in Hospitals

As mentioned earlier, simply becoming a patient in a hospital has its risks. Doctors and nurses know all too well what they are, but patients seldom hear about them until they are the victims. And then, often, they may not realize their hospitalization was the cause.

What kinds of risks? For one thing, you could develop an infection you didn't have when you were admitted, as 5 to 10 percent of hospital patients do (and some 3 percent of those *die* from those infections). Even the cleanest of hospitals are alive with germs, and not just because practically every new patient acts as transport. Hospital staff spread germs, too. If you've seen staff members in "scrub"—the gowns, booties, and caps worn during surgery—eating in the hospital cafeteria, you can pretty well assume that they've been working around somebody who's sick, and that they haven't bothered to remove their now-contaminated garments before heading out for some grub. It's true that such attire might keep them from dribbling spaghetti sauce on their ties, but who knows what germs they're bringing into the cafeteria or trailing down the hall?

When you're examined, you may want to ask the doctor or nurse to wash his or her hands before touching you. The Institute for Child Health reports that many hospital workers

Want Advice from a Nationally Known Obstetrics and Gynecology Staff? Start Here.

These hospitals have worldwide reputations in research and innovation in gynecology or breast cancer. You may want to refer to them for a second opinion.

The Johns Hopkins Hospital
Department of Gynecology and Obstetrics
600 North Wolfe Street
Baltimore, Maryland 21205
1-301-955-5000

This is one of the country's leading programs in the treatment and diagnosis of infertility and reproductive disorders, including in vitro fertilization, gynecologic oncology, gynecologic urodynamics, and high-risk obstetrical consultation.

Brigham and Women's Hospital
Department of Obstetrics and Gynecology
75 Francis Street
Boston, Massachusetts 02115
1-617-732-5500

This teaching affiliate of the Harvard Medical School, one of Boston's most popular hospitals, has one of the largest obstetrics and gynecology services in the country. Menopause, breast cancer, infertility, and high-risk pregnancy are just some of the many medical problems treated here. The medical/surgical staff includes innovators in lumpectomy for breast cancer, immunotherapy for cancer, and postmenopausal hormone replacement therapy.

Massachusetts General Hospital
(Vincent Memorial Hospital)
32 Fruit Street
Boston, Massachusetts 02114
1-617-726-2000

Vincent Memorial, the women's hospital within this world-famous institution, specializes in the treatment of gynecologic cancer, infertility, and other women's diseases. It also has a unique primary care and clinical research program, Women's Health Associates, that provides comprehensive care.

Memorial Sloan-Kettering Hospital
1275 York Avenue
New York, New York 10021
1-212-794-7722

Perhaps the most famous of the cancer hospitals, Sloan-Kettering has a large breast cancer section and experts who provide state-of-the-art treatment even for rare cancers. Patients are admitted to this hospital only if it's determined that they will get better treatment here. This hospital's pain service is considered a model for other hospitals that must treat patients with the often intractable pain associated with cancer.

(continued)

University McDonald Women's Hospital (of the University Hospitals of Cleveland)
2074 Abington Road
Cleveland, Ohio 44106
1-216-844-1000

This hospital specializes in hormone replacement therapy after ovary removal or menopause, infertility, and gynecologic oncology and breast cancer. Wulf Utian, M.D., director of obstetrics and gynecology at University McDonald Women's Hospital, is founder of the North American Society for Menopause Research.

University of Chicago Hospitals (Chicago Lying-In Hospital)
5841 S. Maryland Avenue
Chicago, Illinois 60637
1-312-702-1000

Doctors here specialize in research and treatment of ovarian, vaginal, and vulvar cancer, and are expert in the treatment of cancer caused by exposure to diethylstilbestrol (DES).

Columbia-Presbyterian Medical Center
Department of Obstetrics and Gynecology
or
Department of Gynecologic Pathology
630 West 168th Street
New York, New York 10032
1-212-305-2500

Researchers and clinicians at this hospital specialize in the diagnosis and treatment of sexually transmitted venereal warts caused by the human papilloma virus (HPV). Some strains of this virus can lead to cervical cancer. Expert colposcopy, cervical biopsy, viral typing, second opinion on pathology reports, and laser treatment of cervical warts are available here.

Los Angeles County—University of Southern California Medical Center Women's Hospital
1240 N. Mission Road
Los Angeles, California 90033
1-213-226-2622

This hospital has one of the country's leading programs in reproductive endocrinology and the treatment of menopause.

Medical College of Georgia Hospitals and Clinics
Donald M. Sherline, M.D., Chairman
Department of Obstetrics and Gynecology
Augusta, Georgia 30912
1-404-721-3591

Specializing in hormone replacement and reproductive endocrinology, doctors here are some of the few in the United States involved in research and clinical use of male hormones in women after ovary removal or menopause.

Albert Einstein College of Medicine
Chairman, Department of Obstetrics and Gynecology
1300 Morris Park Avenue
Bronx, New York 10475
1-212-430-4000

This hospital is one of the few in the United States involved in research and clinical use of nutrients such as folate and vitamin A in the treatment of cervical cell abnormalities.

Women's Clinics

The first women's health care clinics were started in the 1960s by women concerned about the abuses of male-dominated medicine and the availability of safe abortions. These clinics' intention, to give women control of their own health care, eventually affected many aspects of medicine, as passive "patients" got smart and began to think like medical consumers. Some of these original women's clinics still operate—the Elizabeth Blackwell Health Center for Women in Philadelphia, the Emma Goldman Health Center for Women in Iowa City, the Vermont Women's Health Center in Burlington, and others.

But don't confuse these places with the "womancare" centers of the 1980s and early 1990s. Although they may provide some of the same services, many of these new centers have a very different philosophy. They exist to make money, not just for themselves but for the hospitals with which they are frequently associated. Medical business journals make it clear that bottom-line-conscious hospital administrators see women's medicine as a high-profile profit-maker, and they see women's health care centers as a way to draw that business in, as patients are referred to the hospital for mammograms, osteoporosis screening, and surgical procedures. There's nothing wrong with patronizing such a center, but don't assume that it offers better care or that its motives are altruistic. Don't let slick marketing or pastel wallpaper lull you into believing you don't need to do your homework. Check it out the same way you'd check out an individual gynecologist. Find out who's on staff and get their credentials. Beware of being overtreated.

who come in direct contact with patients don't take the time, or are not concerned enough, to take this simple precautionary measure. And doctors are among the worst offenders. In two intensive care units studied, hands were washed after patient contact less than half the time. And if your doctor or nurse is wearing rubber gloves and a gown, you want to make sure these items have been donned just prior to entering your room, not three patients previously. So ask. Better the doctor or nurse be offended by your request than for you to suffer additional illness because of their laxness.

Hospital Clinics

Hospital clinics can be lifesavers for women who just don't have the money to see a private doctor. But such clinics are classrooms for eager gynecologists-in-training ("residents") who may want to hone their surgical skills on your innards, whether or not you need an operation. Here, as anywhere, it's vitally important to question any recommended treatment or surgery, even if you have to interrupt a fast-talking doctor to do so. Ask:

● What do you think is wrong with me?

● What do you hope to find in the results of this test?

● Why do you think I need this procedure (or surgery)?

● What are my alternatives?

● What will happen if I don't have this procedure (or surgery)?

Sometimes clinic doctors will suggest what they call "definitive," or conclusive, treatment because they are concerned that you won't be responsible enough to return to the clinic for important follow-up care should they suggest a less aggressive approach. For instance, one might suggest a hysterectomy for simple cervical dysplasia, rather than cryosurgery to remove the abnormal cells and then regular Pap smears to make sure the condition hasn't returned. Prejudices aside, it's up to you to prove you are responsible by asking questions, making your own decisions, and then following through on your medical treatment.

Find out ahead of time if your doctor intends to use a urinary catheter, a flexible tube inserted through the urethra into the bladder to drain urine, during your procedure or operaton. Urinary catheters are a common cause of bladder infections, and they are the source of 40 percent of all infections acquired during a hospital stay.

Some doctors routinely, and unnecessarily, catheterize their female patients, even during minor procedures, when a trip to the bathroom before the procedure would work just as well. Request that you empty your bladder yourself. *Do* expect to be catheterized, though, if you have surgery that involves a large abdominal incision. Ask to have the catheter removed as soon as you are moving around enough to be able to urinate on your own. If you have to have one in for a few days, make sure the nurse checks its drainage regularly.

Surgical wounds account for another 25 percent of hospital-acquired infections, but some hospitals, and some doctors, have lower infection rates than normal, and some have higher. Ask your surgeon her rate of infection for the procedure she's performing on you. Then ask if that rate is high, low, or average. If she doesn't know, ask her to find out for you.

Hospitals are also notorious places for slips, slides, and high-impact landings. Accidental falls are one of the top reasons that patients sue hospitals. The causes? Slippery, wet floors; tripping over IV stands and other medical equipment; sedated patients who shouldn't be standing alone; attempts to crawl out of bed over siderails when a nurse fails to answer a call for help. That's why you should bring rubber-soled slippers with you, and never walk, even if it's just to the bathroom, if you feel faint or groggy.

Drug mix-ups occur regularly in hospitals. According to Kenneth Barker, a pharmacist at Auburn University, hospitals with the best drug-problem records make mistakes 2 to 3 percent of the time. In a three-hundred-bed hospital, this means sixty to ninety drug errors take place every day. And the worst hospitals make up to 11 percent errors. For patients, this may mean receiving the wrong medication, the wrong dose, or no medication when they're supposed to. It means you should ask, each time, what medication you are being given, and take it only if you're sure it's what's been prescribed by your doctor. (Ask the nurse to check your medical records if you're not sure.) And if you're expecting a pill or injection, and don't get it, ask why.

Unnecessary medical testing flourishes in hospitals. Why? Some hospitals require that certain tests be done on every patient admitted, whether or not that test is necessary or has recently been done on the same patient. In some hospitals, doctors reorder the same tests you had before you were admitted; they want to see what results the hospital lab delivers. Consultants may order additional tests; your own doctor may order tests to protect himself in case of a malpractice suit or in a blind attempt to diagnose your illness, not knowing what he's looking for in a result but hoping to find a clue.

Doctors Gone Bad

Although more bad doctors are being disciplined by their state medical boards or having their malpractice insurance terminated by insurance companies (which can force them out of some hospitals, but not private practice), plenty of incompetent, impaired, and immoral doctors are still practicing medicine. Some are poorly trained, or working beyond their skills or area of expertise; some are alcoholics or drug addicts; some are emotionally disturbed; some are senile.

Gynecologists apparently are no more likely than any other kind of doctor to be incompetent, impaired, or immoral. There is no proof, for instance, that they are more prone to sexual misconduct than any other kind of doctor, even though they might have more opportunities to misbehave if they were so inclined. Investigators do admit that sexual harassment or assault is harder to prove than alcoholism or drug abuse, because often the only evidence is the patient's direct testimony. Frequently, it comes down to the patient's word versus the doctor's, and it's up to authorities to decide who to believe. (Of course, the more patients who speak up, the less likely the doctor's story becomes.)

The occasional headline-making case shows just how bizarre some cases of sexual abuse can be. Take the case of Pravin Thakkar, M.D.

This Indiana physician was accused in 1989 of having sexual intercourse with at least one patient while he was doing a pelvic examination, and of aborting the fetuses of that woman and another woman he had impregnated, without their consent or even their knowledge that the painful procedure they were undergoing was an abortion. He allegedly forced other patients into sexual liaisons and coerced them into unneeded breast and pelvic exams.

Sound unbelievable? Some of these women later said they knew something was wrong at the time, but they were too stunned to know what to do. According to United Press International, the woman impregnated on the examining table said that when she later confronted the doctor with the incident and threatened to report him to the authorities, he said, "So go ahead. Who will believe you anyway? You're a housewife, I'm a doctor and have lots of money." She and another woman did eventually file criminal charges. Thakkar's state medical license has been suspended. A hearing to decide whether to renew his license will be held after the criminal charges are resolved.

In another headline-making case, James C. Burt, M.D., of Dayton, Ohio (a.k.a. "Dr. Love"), permanently surrendered his medical license and agreed never to practice medicine again in the United States after being charged in 1989 with

(continued)

74

forty-one violations of ethics or standards.

For years, Burt had been doing experimental vaginal surgery on women, often without their knowledge, after childbirth. He claimed that the surgery was designed to give women more clitoral contact during sexual intercourse, turning them into orgasmic athletes. Unfortunately, the operation turned too many into sexual cripples. Some women developed vaginal scarring and found it too painful to have intercourse; some were plagued by bladder infections, or urinary incontinence, sometimes urinating into the vagina; some had chronic vaginal infections. The operation made vaginal births impossible without undoing all the previous surgery.

How did all this happen? Even though the hospital where Burt operated required patients, from 1979 on, to sign a special consent form that stated that the surgery was "an unproven, nonstandard practice of gynecology," women still didn't understand the possible risks or that the surgery had not been proven to work. They relied on Dr. Burt's reassurances and on his description of the procedure as merely a new combination of standard gynecological surgical procedures, and never sought a second opinion. When they developed problems afterward, says prosecuting attorney Marylee Sambol, many thought it was their body's individual reaction to surgery that had been done correctly. One woman who did file a suit against Burt in 1973 settled out of court because she couldn't find a doctor to testify against Burt.

The response of the medical community in Dayton shows all too well why it's the patient who has to look out for herself. Doctors in Dayton knew about Burt's surgery and "considered it a joke," says attorney Sambol. Even though doctors may have disagreed with what Burt was doing, they were ineffective in limiting his surgical practice. And certainly the hospital where Burt worked profited by allowing him to continue to operate. It took twenty-two years, a national television show exposé, and a good deal of public outcry before Burt lost his license.

Avoiding an incompetent, impaired, or immoral practitioner is not easy. Owning a medical degree and possessing a state-regulated license do not mean that a doctor is able, physically or mentally, to treat you. It means that he has met the requirements of medical education. That doctor still may be an alcoholic or a substance abuser, may be suffering from a severe mental problem, or like Dr. Burt, may be operating well outside the range of accepted medical practice.

That's why you need to ask questions. Ask the questions listed in "Choosing the Doctor," page 2. And listen good. Do the answers make sense? Is the doctor using a lot of mumbo jumbo? Ask more questions: Has his license ever been suspended by a state medical licensing board? Call the board in your *(continued)* state to see if any complaints have been filed or are on record. Ask other doctors, nurses, and health professionals in your community about the doctor. During your get-acquainted visit, or any visit, keep your eyes open. Does the doctor seem distracted? Jumpy? Do his hands shake? Does he avert his eyes when you are talking? Can you smell alcohol on his breath?

Are you uncomfortable with a doctor's behavior toward you? Has he done something to you that you're not sure is part of a standard gynecologic exam? Call the head of obstetrics and gynecology at the nearest medical center or university hospital and ask to discuss this with her. Then decide if you want to file a complaint against that doctor with your state medical licensing board. Remember, your complaint may be the only thing that saves another woman from the same, or even worse, abuse.

———

The problem with all these tests is that, if enough are done, even on a perfectly healthy person, sooner or later some test is bound to show something abnormal. The result may be that you're treated for a condition you don't have, or that a real illness is overlooked. This is why it's more important than ever, if you're admitted to the hospital, to ask the same questions you'd ask before you agree to any test, procedure, or surgery recommended: What you are looking for in the results of this test? Do the benefits of this test outweigh the risks? What do you think will happen if I don't have this test?

Check with your doctor to make sure that a test or retest is necessary, and why. Don't allow yourself to be whisked away by some attendant for another test unless you are absolutely sure you should be having it. If a test needs to be done over and over, call a halt. The problem may be an inept technician or faulty equipment. If you desire a second opinion on interpretation of test results, ask your doctor to find you an independent expert outside of the hospital. Otherwise your "second opinion" might come from the same person who gave the first report, or a fellow employee who might not want to contradict a co-worker.

CHAPTER THREE

A Typical Visit to the Gynecologist

By now you've either selected a gynecologist or decided to stay with the one you already have. You have some knowledge about how gynecologists are trained and the areas in which they're not trained. You know that, like other doctors, gynecologists tend to discount women's physical pain or assume it's psychological. You know there's always a chance that your doctor will recommend tests or surgery you may not need, or that he'll fail to follow up on a symptom that requires treatment. You realize how important it is to ask questions, and to keep asking until you get clear answers. You've had a get-acquainted visit with this doctor and decided he's the one for you. You scheduled a routine pelvic examination and Pap smear. Now it's time for that appointment.

A woman's first-ever gynecologic exam is a scary, awkward, and momentous-enough occasion that many women can remember it in detail. And not a few women experience at least some embarrassment and fear every time they see the gynecologist. Even the position, on your back with your legs spread, in the air, is about as vulnerable as most people care to get. It's a time when you really want to be able to trust whoever's down there, working away. The last thing you need is to be surprised by some cold instrument or sudden jab. (Ever wonder why you put your feet in those metal stirrups? It's so you can't kick the doctor in the head if he hurts you.) A sheet, draped over your knees, may provide warmth and modesty, but if you want to see the doctor's face as he works and talks (to your crotch), you can either push the sheet down or remove it.

If this *is* your first visit to the gynecologist, you may want to admit that when you make your appointment. Why? Because you'll be scheduled for more time than usual, and you should expect special treatment (see "When Should You First See a Gynecologist?", p. 44). If you feel rushed or manhandled during your visit, now is as good a time as any to voice your complaints. If you've had a get-acquainted visit (see "The Get-Acquainted Visit," p. 14) and a chance to look around prior to your exam, you're less likely to be faced with a doctor or a situation you don't like, and you won't be seeing the doctor for the first time in the examining room, when you're undressed. It's natural to feel somewhat uneasy during this first exam, but it's always possible that something is amiss. (Doctors are human, too, and one out of ten suffers from drug addiction, alcohol abuse, or mental illness. And some do fondle or sexually abuse their patients.) Remember, it's your right to have a female nurse present, to refuse the exam or to schedule it for later, to insist that it stop, even if it's already started, and to get up and leave.

Even if this is a routine visit, take some time to think about possible hidden agendas—things in the back of your mind that are bothering you but that you might be afraid or embarrassed to ask the doctor about. Are you wondering if you should be tested for AIDS? Do you want to know what treatments are available for premenstrual syndrome? Do you think you may have symptoms of menopause? And come prepared to answer questions about your medical and reproductive history. (Now is the time to ask family members about illnesses that may not have been discussed much, or that were only hinted at as "female problems.") These questions may address the following issues:

- Your family's history of breast cancer (See page 198)
  If your mother, sisters, or grandmothers had breast cancer, especially before age forty-five, or in both breasts, your own risks for developing breast cancer are higher than normal. Your doctor may recommend mammogram screening at an earlier-

than-usual age and urge you to practice regular breast self-exam. She may be much more aggressive in diagnosing any breast lumps you develop, even if you are young and appear to have only a fluid-filled cyst.

- Your family's history of cancer of the reproductive organs
  Neither cervical or endometrial cancer appears to be related to genetics. But one of the most deadly female cancers, ovarian cancer, can run in families. The normal risk of this disease is one in seventy, or 1.4 percent. If two or more first-degree relatives have it, however, your odds jump to 50 percent. Some doctors recommend that women with a strong family history of ovarian cancer have their ovaries removed at age thirty-five just to be safe. But most simply monitor the ovaries with a painless ultrasound probe inserted into the vagina and by feeling the ovaries with their fingers, through the vagina and rectum, as is done in a regular pelvic examination.

- The date of your last menstrual period (the month and year, if you are past menopause); the number of days in your cycle (average is twenty-eight); the number of days you usually have your period (average is five); the amount of flow (light, moderate, or heavy, usually calculated by the number of tampons or sanitary napkins you use); symptoms that might indicate a problem: pain, swelling, fever, unusual discharge, or bleeding.

- The number of children you have; their ages; any miscarriages, abortions, or stillbirths; if you have been attempting without success to become pregnant, and for how long.

- Whether you are using birth control, and if so, what kind and if you are having any problems with it

- Whether you have ever had sexually transmitted diseases, such as venereal warts, genital herpes, or *chlamydia*, and if so, when

- Questions about your general health (your bowels, urinary tract, circulatory system) and your mental health (whether you've been anxious or depressed, whether you are taking tranquilizers or other psychoactive drugs). The American College of Obstetrics and Gynecology says the exam should include taking an "emotional history," which, apparently, gynecologists interpret many different ways. "I always ask a woman if she likes herself, and I always ask anyone over age twenty how's her sex life," one male doctor says. Another gynecologist, a woman, says she'd find such questions offensive and unnecessary. If you feel that the doctor is being insensitive or flippant, or is showing an unwarranted interest in your sex life, ask why he is posing a particular question. If his response doesn't suit you, tell him you prefer not to answer.

An ideal gynecological exam, according to the American College of Obstetricians and Gynecologists, will also include checking your weight and blood pressure, taking a urine sample to check for signs of diabetes or a bladder infection, and taking blood to check for anemia. (Many of the gynecologists we talked with, though, said they do urine or blood tests only if a woman has symptoms such as urinary urgency, which could indicate a bladder infection, or heavy bleeding or fatigue, which could point toward anemia.)

Next you'll be asked to undress and put on a hospital gown. (You may also want to urinate, if you weren't asked for a urine sample. The exam can put pressure on your bladder, making you feel the need to go.) Then you'll wait—briefly, one would hope—sitting either on the edge of the examining table or in a chair in the examining room, for the doctor. (If you get chilly, request a blanket.)

When the doctor arrives, she should greet you and introduce herself, if this is the first you're seeing her since you arrived in the office. The doctor will go over your medical history with you and ask additional questions where necessary.

Then you'll lie down on the examining table, and the doctor will check your breasts for lumps. (She'll ask you to slip your gown down over one shoulder at a time to expose each breast.) She should be looking for asymmetry, puckering, and changes in the nipple and skin texture. She'll feel your breasts, circling with her fingertips. She should also feel around your armpits and your collarbone, places where early breast cancer can spread. She should gently squeeze your breasts to see if she can express fluid from the nipple. (Some kinds of breast fluid need to be examined for signs of early cancer.) She should ask if you do breast self-exam. If you don't, she should ask if you want instruction, and either show you herself or have a nurse show you, give you a pamphlet, or arrange for you to view an instructional videotape during your visit.

The doctor should also check your thyroid gland, at the base of your neck, for enlargement or nodules, and palpate your abdomen. That means she'll press down lightly with her fingertips to feel the size and consistency of your internal organs, including your liver and spleen.

Then it's on to the pelvic exam. For this, you'll be asked to bend your legs and put your feet into metal semicircles—stirrups—which will raise your feet about eighteen inches above your body. Then you'll be asked to slide your body down toward the end of the examining table, until you're in a kind of squatting position, but lying on your back. It does feel like a very vulnerable position, and it is. (It's also a position that a male doctor has probably never assumed in his life, particularly with his pants off.) Since your gown will most likely fall back onto your belly in this position, a paper sheet will be draped over your bare legs. If you want to be able to see the doctor's face, as she does the exam, either push the sheet down between your legs or ask that it be removed. (If the doctor asks why, just say it's because you want to be able to see her.) If you are unable to assume this position, perhaps because you have arthritis in your hips, the doctor should be able to examine you lying on your side with your knees drawn up toward your chest.

The doctor should wear surgical gloves for this part of the exam. She'll start by visually examining the external genitals for irritation, herpes sores, genital warts, or anything else unusual. She'll do this by gently spreading the folds of skin around your vagina.

Next she'll insert into your vagina an instrument called a speculum. This metal or plastic device resembles a duckbill with a handle. It comes in about four sizes, with blades from three to six inches long. The doctor will choose a speculum size based on your age and size, and she should select the smallest size if you have never been sexually active. The blades are slowly inserted into the vagina and then locked open about an inch apart. This allows the doctor to look from the outside in, at your cervix, and to insert and withdraw instruments without touching the sides of your vagina. Most doctors run warm water over the speculum to warm and lubricate it before inserting it. Other lubricants should not be used during this part of the exam, since they can ruin the Pap smear. A speculum may look incredibly large to someone who's never seen one before. ("Some girls take one look at it and say, 'No way,'" Dr. Gidwani admits. That's why she doesn't show it to every patient.) But the fact is, although the speculum may cause a sensation of pressure, it rarely hurts, even in virgins. Your doctor would have to be using much too large a speculum, opening it way too wide, or you'd have to have sores in your vagina, or be very tense, for this part of the exam to hurt. If you are concerned, ask your doctor what size speculum she intends to use. Ask to see it. Ask her to open it up and lock it in place so you can see how big it will be when it's in your vagina. Ask her if it's the smallest size available. Ask her to agree to withdraw it if you experience any pain. Long slow breaths can help you relax.

With the speculum in place, the doctor can see your cervix, the neck of your uterus, which extends into the vagina. She'll look for redness, discharge, and rough spots, which could mean precancerous cell changes.

Then she'll do a Pap smear ("Pap" is short for Papanicolaou, the doctor who devised this test to detect abnormal cell changes). She'll use a pipe-cleaner-type brush, a wooden spatula, or a long cotton-tip swab to gently scrape cells from your cervix. She may take a second sample of cells from your upper vagina if she thinks you have a vaginal infection or if you have been exposed to DES (see p. 138). She'll smear the cells onto a glass slide and spray the slide with a fixative, a chemical that preserves the cells' present state. The slide will be sent to a laboratory where it will be examined under a microscope for signs of cancer, infection, and inflammation.

As the doctor withdraws the speculum, she may slightly turn and rotate it so that she can examine the sides of your vagina for infection. This, too, generally is painless.

Next the doctor will insert two gloved, lubricated fingers into the vagina until they are against the cervix. Then, with her other hand, she will press on your abdomen, feeling the size and shape of your uterus and checking for masses that might be on your ovaries or fallopian tubes. Here again you will feel pressure, and you will probably also feel some pinching pain as the doctor feels your ovaries. ("I tell male doctors it is the equivalent of having their testicles squeezed," Dr. Gidwani says.) One ovary may be particularly sensitive to touch if you are midcycle and ovulating.

Finally, the doctor may insert one finger into your rectum and one into your vagina. This makes it easier for her to feel your ovaries, which lie slightly behind the uterus, toward the rectum. It's also the only way to check an area called the cul-de-sac, a space between the vagina and rectum that can harbor endometriosis, abscesses, and tumors. And it allows her to check your rectum for precancerous growths (polyps) or hemorrhoids, and to do a stool blood test with the small amount of feces that may collect on the glove. Not all doctors include a rectal exam in their gynecologic exam, so you may want to ask ahead if this is something your doctor does. Some women find the rectal exam more unpleasant than the vaginal exam.

Even on a routine visit, you should have plenty of time to ask questions: before the exam begins, during it, and afterward. The doctor should tell you what she is doing each step of the way, every time. Many doctors (and especially those who teach gynecology) say they also tell their patients what they are finding as they do the exam, rather than waiting until it's all over. This way the patient is usually reassured during the exam, or, if a problem is seen or felt, the patient knows exactly why the doctor is taking extra time on a particular part of her body. If your doctor is not providing this information as she does the exam, ask her to describe what she is doing and finding: What are you doing now? What are you feeling? How does my cervix look? Does my uterus feel normal? Do my ovaries feel normal?

After the exam, if everything appears normal, the doctor may simply say you'll be called in about two weeks if the results of your Pap smear are abnormal. She should ask if you have any additional questions. If she does find a problem, she should have you get dressed and meet with her in her office to discuss it. (Let her know if you don't want to talk while perched on an examining table in a flimsy paper gown.)

As you leave the office, you'll be asked if you would like to make an appointment for next year, or for whatever time interval the doctor has recommended. You'll also be told once again that you'll be notified if your Pap smear is abnormal. It's a good idea, however, to call the office yourself in about two weeks to find out the results. Why? Because doctor's offices have been known to fail to contact patients about abnormal Pap smear results. Don't assume yours is normal. Know for sure.

What If You're Seeing the Gynecologist for a Problem?

Most women who see a gynecologist regularly for routine care soon fall into a fairly comfortable pattern. They learn what to expect during a visit, and, if they're smart medical consumers, they also learn what questions to ask. Their yearly visit for a Pap smear and pelvic and breast exams may be as short as ten or fifteen minutes, and their gynecologist may not remember them as individuals from year to year. (If he does, maybe it's because all those questions have left a lasting impression!)

If the routine varies, it may be because you need to make extra visits to the doctor for a vaginal infection or a sexually transmitted disease; for pregnancy, abortion, or a change in birth control method; for problems associated with menopause; or perhaps even for symptoms that point toward cancer.

In any case, to a greater or lesser degree, the visit is no longer routine, for you or for the doctor. It will take longer; it will involve new questions, and possibly tests, to pinpoint the cause of your symptoms. It may include recommendations for treatment, referral to a specialist, or even the suggestion of surgery. You may be upset and find it hard to explain things or to think about what questions you need to ask, much less ask them. And if the answers seem to be bad news, you may have trouble comprehending what the doctor is saying. (That's why it's a good idea to bring along a tape recorder. Explain to the doctor that you are not recording this with the intent of suing him, but rather to keep track of what he says.)

And your doctor himself may not be sure what's going on, so he may not be able to answer your question: "What's wrong with me?" What needs to happen now is for you and your doctor to discuss what he thinks your health problem may be (or even what *you* think it might be) and the diagnostic process your doctor wants to use to find out for sure. Not all doctors are used to sharing their diagnostic process with patients. And some, certainly, see no need to explain such things.

That's why you need to ask questions, including some very specific and important questions that apply to any medical problem. Such probing may well be the only way you'll obtain information you need to make wise decisions about your medical care.

Let's follow one smart traveler, "Mary Smith," through her visit to the gynecologist for a problem.

At age forty-eight, Mary is approaching menopause. Her periods have become somewhat irregular, but they haven't stopped. Suddenly Mary starts having an occasional, very heavy period, and episodes of spotting between periods. The third time this happens she makes an appointment with her gynecologist. She is very concerned. Are these normal symptoms of menopause? What if she has cancer? What else could it be? Will her doctor say she needs a hysterectomy? The kinds of questions she asks herself, and her doctor, will help her use her own common sense to get the kind of information she needs to make an informed decision.

Is a gynecologist the kind of doctor I should be seeing for this problem?

Mary has both a family doctor and a gynecologist. She hasn't needed to see her family doctor for some time; in fact, as her children get older, she sees him less and less. But she did see her gynecologist nine months earlier, and she has seen him about once a year for the last eight years for routine care. To her the gynecologist seems like the obvious choice. After all, he *does* specialize in women's reproductive organs. For other problems, though, such as a urinary tract infection, breast lump, or pelvic pain, she might use her family doctor.

Is it an emergency? Am I very worried?

Mary knows she isn't going to bleed to death if she doesn't see her doctor today, so she doesn't consider her problem an emergency. But she also knows she is worried enough that she wants to see the doctor as soon as possible. And she realizes she would be upset if she is told she has to wait longer than three days for an appointment. She is prepared to argue for an earlier appointment if necessary (and to ask to be called if someone else cancels hers). Because her doctor works in a group practice, she is also ready to accept an appointment with one of his colleagues, a woman doctor she has seen a few times when her regular doctor was unavailable.

■ *What is my doctor going to want to know about my problem?*

By checking her appointment calendar, Mary is able to reconstruct the onset and progress of her symptoms (and she brings the calendar along with her). She knows her medical record at the doctor's office lists the date of her last pelvic examination and the results of her most recent Pap smear. Is she under stress? She wasn't, any more than usual, until this abnormal bleeding started! If he asks, Mary knows she'll tell her doctor that she believes this is strictly a physical problem.

Mary's visit includes a careful medical history, a pelvic exam, and a Pap smear, because she hasn't had one in almost a year. While doing the exam, her doctor reports that her cervix appears to look normal, and that her uterus is its normal size and shape. He also notes that he is able to feel her ovaries and that they both feel normal.

He explains that although he is doing a Pap smear, this test is accurate only for detecting cancer of the cervix. "It's not a reliable test for detecting cancer of the ovaries, uterus, or, especially, of the uterine lining, the endometrium," he says. "We need to do another test or two to get to the bottom of this."

Even though Mary is thinking to herself, "Sure, I want to get to the bottom of this, too," that's *not* what she says to her doctor! She doesn't automatically agree to every test her doctor suggests.

Why? Because she knows that studies show doctors frequently order tests that are unnecessary, inappropriate, and costly. Doctors rely too much on the results of tests that may be inaccurate and too little on their clinical judgment. They order tests to confirm a diagnosis they have already made; as a blind guess when they have no idea what illness you have; as protection in case they're sued for malpractice; or because they or the hospital have just bought a costly diagnostic doodad that needs to earn its keep. Wouldn't you agree with Mary that these are poor reasons to undergo what might be a painful, even a dangerous, procedure? She agrees to nothing until her doctor has answered some important questions to her satisfaction.

So Mary asks:

▬ *What tests?*

In her case, her doctor suggests, for starters, an endometrial biopsy. He explains what it is: a sampling of tissue taken from the uterine lining which will be examined under a microscope for signs of abnormal growth.

▬ *How is this test done?*

Mary's doctor says there are several ways to do an endometrial biopsy, and that the method he uses is common, accurate, and less painful than procedures used in the past. He'll place a speculum in her vagina, swab her cervix to disinfect it, then insert a thin plastic tube through her cervix and into her uterus. Then he'll pull a plunger on the end of the tube to create suction, which will draw a bit of endometrial tissue into the tube. He'll be able to sample all sides of the uterus by rotating the tube 360 degrees and continuing the suction as he withdraws the tube.

Mary asks questions until she can visualize the whole process, start to finish. How big is this tube? Can I see it? How far into my uterus will you put it? How will you know when to stop? How much tissue will you remove?

▬ *Will it hurt?*

Mary's doctor hesitates for a moment before he answers this one. He knows the perception of pain varies from person to person. And, of course, he has never had the procedure done on himself. He's never had a menstrual cramp. Heck, he doesn't even have a uterus! "Well," he says, "it's not painless. Some women tell me they have cramping and moderate pain, but that's about it. And the pain lasts probably less than a minute. I've never had a patient faint during the procedure, or insist that I stop." He also explains that although he could inject a numbing anesthesia into her cervix to lessen the pain, the injections hurt as much as the procedure and take longer to do, so he doesn't like to use them.

■ *Is it dangerous?*

By this time Mary's doctor realizes she won't settle for a simple "Of course not." So he says, "When we used to use a metal tube for this procedure there was some risk that the doctor would puncture the uterus. Now that we use flexible plastic tubes, that doesn't happen. There is a slight risk of infection, just as there is anytime a surgical instrument is inserted into the uterus. But any infection can be treated; it's not life-threatening."

■ *Will you do this procedure yourself?*

"Yes, I can do it myself, right here in my office, right now."

"Not so fast. I've got a few more questions. How often do you perform this procedure? What is your complication rate? Do you have privileges to do this same procedure in a hospital?" When her doctor tells her that he performs this procedure three or four times a week, that he has a complication rate slightly lower than average, and that the procedure is too minor to necessitate hospital privileges, Mary is reassured that he is capable of doing the procedure. But she's not yet ready to consent.

■ *What will you be looking for in the results of this test?*

This is a crucial question. It makes your gynecologist explain his thinking to you—the process he follows to come up with a diagnosis, a process both of elimination and of confirmation.

"I suspect that you may have some form of endometrial hyperplasia," her doctor says. "That's a condition where the cells that form the lining of the uterus grow rapidly and some-times undergo abnormal changes that can lead to cancer. This test will tell me whether or not you have that condition, and in what form. It's definitely the first test I would do, and it may be the only test we need to do. It will give me valuable infor-mation about the possible causes of your abnormal bleeding, and the kind of treatment you may need."

■ *Should I get a second opinion?*

"You're certainly welcome to do that anytime you want," Mary's doctor says, "but this is not a particularly painful, dan-gerous, time-consuming, or costly procedure, and at this time, I don't think it's necessary."

■ *How much time will it take to do this test?*

This might seem like a trivial question, but right now Mary is thinking about whether she'll have to take time off from work to come in for this test, and perhaps, to come in later to discuss the results of the test, if she doesn't have it done during this visit, and for treatment. It's just one more bit of infor-mation that might weigh against having a test, if the test is of questionable diagnostic value.

"Since you're here and I can do it right now, it will only take a few minutes," her doctor says. "If you decide to think about this for a few days, you'll have to schedule another ap-pointment, and the whole thing could take half an hour, al-though the actual procedure itself takes only a minute or two."

■ *How much will it cost?*

"Don't worry, your insurance will cover it" is her doctor's first answer. "But I want to know anyway," Mary replies. Like many physicians, Mary's doctor has no idea how much this procedure costs. When his billing clerk looks up the charge, even he is surprised to find out how expensive it is. "That's the standard rate," his billing clerk insists. Mary makes a mental note to ask some other gynecologists their charge for this service.

■ *Do the potential benefits outweigh the risks?*

"Well, we know the benefit of this test," Mary's doctor says. "It will tell us whether or not you have a condition that could become life-threatening cancer. I think that's a great potential benefit. And we know the risks—infection of the uterus. We know that risk is slight, and that if it occurs, it can be treated. I personally believe the potential benefits of this test outweigh the risks."

■ *What do you think will happen if I don't have this test?*

Mary's doctor is very clear about this. "I think you will probably continue to have a problem with abnormal bleeding. And I am worried that you could develop endometrial cancer, a condition that, left untreated, could require that you have a hysterectomy, or that could threaten your life. I don't think this will go away by itself, or that it is something you can ignore."

By asking questions, Mary has gotten quite a bit of information, in a logical fashion, from her doctor regarding her medical problem. It's information her doctor might not have volunteered otherwise.

Whether or not she wanted it, she has also gotten her doctor's opinion about what she should do. But because of her questions, she can see his opinion as a choice, possibly the best choice, but not as her only option.

Based on her medical history and physical examination, Mary's doctor prescribes a hormone, progesterone, that day, to help regulate her menstrual cycles and ensure complete shedding of the endometrial lining each month. Because she knows that doctors sometimes prescribe drugs that are unnecessary and can cause serious side effects, including death, Mary asks more questions. She wants to make sure the drug her doctor is prescribing is necessary and the best choice among the possible drugs she could take for her problem.

■ *What is this drug? What is it supposed to do?*

The doctor gives her both the brand name and the generic name of the drug. He tells her it is a synthetic (laboratory-made) version of progesterone, a female hormone secreted by the ovaries. He tells her how the drug will work in her body, supplementing her low levels of progesterone to ensure a normal menstrual cycle.

■ *How long has this drug been on the market?*

Mary knows new drugs are required by the U.S. Food and Drug Administration to be tested before they are given approval to be marketed, but that new drugs sometimes have unforeseen side effects. Since older drugs have survived a shakedown period, their side effects are generally known. But an older drug may not work as well as a newer drug. And it may have more side effects. The doctor tells her that this drug has been on the market for at least thirty years, and has had a safe record.

■ *What are the side effects of this drug?*

Mary knows that almost every drug has some side effects, some severe. Her doctor tells her some of the most common, and severe but rare, side effects of the drug he is prescribing. Mary also makes a mental note to ask her pharmacist for an information sheet that lists indications for use, and side effects, of the drug. She wants to make sure the benefits of taking the drug outweigh the risks, that there's no safer drug, or nondrug treatment, that would work just as well.

■ *How should this drug be taken?*

Mary's doctor explains how she should take it, and says he'll include the same instructions with the pills. (See "Safe and Unsafe Drugs for Women," p. 171.)

Mary decides to wait on the endometrial biopsy. She goes to the medical library at a nearby hospital to read up on the subject; she also consults some women's health books and talks with some friends about it. One refers her to another friend who had the same problem.

Within a week, she has the endometrial biopsy. The results show that she is indeed low in progesterone, and that she has mild endometrial hyperplasia. After six months of progesterone treatment, she has another biopsy. By this time her endometrium has returned to normal. She stays on progesterone therapy for two more years. Then her periods end. She has reached menopause. Her doctor offers her hormone replacement therapy—both estrogen and progesterone—but so far Mary has decided she feels fine without hormones.

So, again, let's review Mary's important questions to her doctor, and why they should be asked:

■ *Is a gynecologist the doctor I should be seeing for this problem?*

In some cases, like Mary's, the appropriateness of seeing a gynecologist may seem obvious. They *do* specialize in women's reproductive organs. For other problems, though, such as a urinary tract infection, breast lump, or pelvic pain, a family doctor or internist are as likely choices.

All three will do an initial assessment and provide treatment or referrals to other doctors when necessary. You may choose to call the doctor you see most often. If your gynecologist is your only doctor (your primary care physician) and you have a problem in which he has no expertise, say, chest pain, you may want to ask for a referral by phone rather than wasting time and money on an office visit. Your doctor should be willing to give you the name of another doctor over the phone, and tell you to inform the new doctor that your gynecologist referred you.

■ *Is it an emergency? Am I very worried?*

How you talk with the gynecologist's receptionist or office manager may determine how soon you get to see the doctor. You don't want to "cry wolf," but you also don't want to spend endless anxious days waiting for an appointment because you didn't express your urgency.

Tell the office manager your concerns. If she says she can't or won't fit you in as soon as you desire, maybe your doctor is just too busy to suit you. Maybe you need to find a new doctor. (Or maybe your doctor needs to find a new office manager. You may ask to speak with him directly.)

■ *What is my doctor going to want to know about my problem?*

During your visit, be prepared to recount the history of your medical problem: when you first noticed it, whether it's been getting worse, any pain, any other symptoms. When did you last have a pelvic examination and Pap smear? Was your Pap smear normal? (Don't forget, though, that the Pap smear is a highly inaccurate test.) Are you taking any drugs? Have you been under stress?

■ *What test (or procedure)? How is this test (or procedure) done?*

Get the exact name of the test or procedure, and find out step by step how it's done. If it's a tissue sample, does it involve scraping, cutting, or using a "punch" to get the tissue? How big a piece of tissue is going to be removed? If it's some sort of X ray or scan, does it involve injecting radioactive solutions or opaque dyes into your body? Are you going to have to be anesthetized? Tranquilized? Cut open? Will the doctor insert a catheter into your bladder? Ask enough questions so you can visualize the test. You may even want to go to a medical library and read about the procedure in a gynecology textbook. Some textbooks also have lots of photographs of procedures and operations, but they can be scary-looking, so be prepared.

■ *Will it hurt? Is it dangerous?*

Don't hesitate to ask these questions. They aren't silly, and the answers will help you weigh the risks and benefits of the test. Some doctors, and especially gynecologists, it seems, tend to minimize pain and danger, perhaps thinking their female patients will fare better if they are spared these details. They may or may not, but the choice should be the patient's.

You may decide that a fairly painful procedure that lasts

only a few minutes may be tolerable, especially if the alternative is a stay in the hospital with general anesthesia and all its accompanying risks. And you may want to ask the doctor, up front, if he'll stop the procedure if your pain becomes too much, or if he can give you a pain reliever to take before the procedure.

Every surgical procedure has its risks and possible complications. Ask your doctor to explain exactly what these risks are, and how likely they are to occur with the procedure he's recommending for you. Uncontrolled bleeding, infection, accidental perforation of abdominal organs, and anesthesia complications are all possible with invasive tests and minor surgery.

■ *Will you do this test (or procedure) yourself?*

If yes, ask how often he does it and where he does it. In his office? A same-day surgical center? The hospital? What is his complication rate? Does he have privileges to do this same procedure in a hospital? You want to get a feel for how competent your doctor is at doing the test or procedure.

If he's planning to send you to another doctor for the test or procedure, find out why he's picked that doctor. Is it because he's the most skilled person in town for that test or procedure? Or is it because he's the only doctor in town who knows how to do it or who has the equipment?

■ *What will you be looking for in the results of this test?*

Again, this is a crucial question because it makes your gynecologist let you in on what he thinks your diagnosis will be and how he intends to pursue it. Mary's doctor knew what medical condition he was looking for—endometrial hyperplasia. And, luckily, he had access to an accurate and fairly simple test that could confirm whether or not Mary had this condition.

If your doctor's response to this question is something like "We won't know until we take a look," call a time-out. If he doesn't know what he is looking for, why has he ordered this test? Some doctors don't like to mention at this point that cancer is a possible diagnosis. If you suspect this is the reason your doctor is being vague, you might want to mention it yourself. Could it be cancer? If the doctor is elusive for other reasons, it might be because you don't really need the test.

■ *Should I get a second opinion?*

If a test is particularly painful, dangerous, time-consuming, or costly, getting a second opinion is a wise move. You may want to obtain it from a doctor with more training than a general gynecologist, such as a gynecologic oncologist or a breast cancer specialist. A different doctor may suggest better or easier ways of diagnosing your health problem.

■ *How much time will it take?*

This might seem like a trivial question. If a test or procedure is of questionable diagnostic value, however, and to have it performed means losing time at work, some much-needed pay, maybe even losing your job, the time is a major consideration.

Will you expect to wait half a day at an outpatient clinic until your turn comes? Will you need multiple visits? And how long will it take to perform the actual test? Answers to these questions will help you determine if you want and can afford to have the test.

■ *How much will it cost?*

If your doctor's answer is "Don't worry, your insurance will cover it," find out what the charge is anyway. If your doctor doesn't know, his billing clerk will. Just because your insurance covers the cost doesn't mean you don't pay—you do, when you pay your share of your insurance premium. And we all pay eventually for America's astronomical annual medical bill. You may want to shop around for the best doctor at the best price.

■ *Do the potential benefits outweigh the risks?*

Ask your doctor to summarize the advantages of having the test (detecting a possibly life-threatening cancer, for example) and the risks (possible perforation of the uterus, a uterine infection, perhaps a reaction to an anesthetic).

This may be the single most important query you can pose

anytime you're faced with a medical decision. Your doctor should be asking it himself, and you'd be wise to ask it anytime a procedure is recommended.

■ *What do you think will happen if I decide not to have this test?*

If your doctor says, "You may die," your desire to have the test (or procedure) could be overwhelming. (You still may want to get a second or even a third opinion first, though.) If your doctor says, "Well, nothing will happen" or "We'll just have to keep an eye on things" or even "I won't be able to make the payment on my Mercedes this month," you may decide you can live without a test and save yourself some time, money, and grief.

If you've come to the conclusion that for every step in your medical care, there are scores of logical, orderly questions that need to be asked, and answered, you're well on your way. You're becoming the kind of medical consumer who understands how sound medical decisions are made. You now know more than many women do about gynecology and gynecologists. And most important, you know what's needed to obtain additional information: questions and more questions.

CHAPTER FOUR

Procedures and Conditions:

All the Facts, from Pap
Smears to Breast
Cancer

I t's easy to be misled when it comes to gynecologic care. Even the most popular procedures are questionable for many women.
The dilemma is that doctors like to be sure,
or at least to give the appearance that they are. They may think
certainty is reassuring to their patients. In fact, it *is* comfort-
ing, but it is false comfort and can be misleading if the real
situation involves uncertainty and controversy. Many areas of
women's health care involve more unknowns and conflicting
findings than many doctors care to admit to their patients. It's
up to you to ask the questions that give you a full understanding of these health concerns.

Pap Smears

For most women, the benefit of routine Pap smears seems
obvious. The test offers the chance to detect cervical cancer
early enough to treat it successfully. Many organizations, including the American Cancer Society and the National Cancer
Institute, recommend periodic or annual Pap smears. Women
who follow these recommendations probably believe they are
doing the best thing they can to prevent cervical cancer. And,
indeed, they may be.

But the fact is, like many other medical screening tests,
the results of a Pap smear are best evaluated with caution.

Even though it's one of the most common cancer screening tests, it's also one of the most inaccurate. The test, as done today, fails to detect 20 to 40 percent of cases of cervical cancer or precursor cell abnormalities. This is something your gynecologist probably hasn't told you.

And even when the Pap smear *is* accurate, the results can create confusion. You may end up being treated for a condition that would have disappeared on its own or at least never developed into cancer. You might even be told you have cancer, or a precancerous condition, not knowing that doctors sometimes disagree on exactly what cervical cell abnormalities fit those categories. All in all, there are lots of good reasons to question your doctor closely about any abnormal Pap smear, and to be wary of any treatment recommended on the basis of a Pap smear alone. It's also important to check out any symptoms of abnormal bleeding even though you've recently had a normal Pap smear.

What Is a Pap Smear?

A Pap smear is a scraping of cells from the cervix, the part of the uterus that extends into the vagina. The cells are collected from the mouth of the cervical canal, a narrow opening into the uterus where cell changes that can lead to cervical cancer are most likely to begin.

The cells are smeared onto a glass slide, sprayed with a fixative to preserve them, and sent to a laboratory to be examined under a microscope for abnormalities. Each smear is classified (see p. 100), and a report of any abnormalities is sent back to the doctor.

Why Is the Pap Smear So Inaccurate?

Doctors' failure to take an adequate cell sample accounts for about half the errors, says the American College of Obstetricians and Gynecologists. Some doctors may be poorly trained; others, simply in a hurry.

Ask your gynecologist if the laboratory she uses sends back inadequate smears, rather than simply reporting them as normal. This is an important way for your doctor to get feedback on how well she is performing her Pap smears. If your doctor uses a cone-shaped "cyto" brush rather than a wooden stick or cotton swab to scrape the cervix, she's also more likely to get a good sampling of cells.

Errors in reading Pap smears at the laboratory account for the other half of the errors.

In 1987, the *Wall Street Journal* investigated the Pap-screening industry. It found high-volume cut-rate laboratories with overworked, undersupervised technicians, many paid on a piecework basis that encouraged them to rush the analysis. They also found that the few laws regulating the industry were often ignored.

Since that time, federal regulations have put a ceiling on the number of Pap smears a lab technician can do per week at labs receiving federal funds or doing interstate business. They have also established proficiency testing and standards to check a lab's error rate. It's too soon to tell whether these laws will improve the quality of Pap smear testing. So it's important to ask your gynecologist these questions:

— *Where will my Pap smear be sent?*

Is the laboratory certified by the College of American Pathologists or the American Society of Cytology? Experts say either of these certifications is most likely to indicate reliability.

If the lab does testing for Medicare or Medicaid patients, chances are it is accredited and has passed an on-site inspection. But this doesn't necessarily give the kind of quality assurance that accreditation by either of the above professional organizations provides, because, apparently, Medicare inspectors don't always know what to look for when they visit a lab. A survey sponsored by the Health Care Financing Administration in 1989 showed that routine Medicare inspections failed to detect potentially serious discrepancies in slide interpretation at eight out of seventeen labs. So don't count on Medicare inspection alone as assurance of a lab's reliability.

99

How You Can Make Your Pap Smear More Accurate

Lubricants, contraceptive foams and jellies, and even semen and blood can mingle with the cells taken during a Pap smear, making it difficult for the lab technician to examine the slide properly. For best results, avoid using these products (and use a condom) for three days before your Pap smear. Schedule your appointment well after your period has ended.

Don't douche for at least three days before your appointment. Douching can wash away the cells your doctor needs to sample.

A Pap smear can identify bacterial and fungal infections such as *candida* and *trichomonas*. An infection can make examination of the slide harder though, because it can obscure precancerous cell abnormalities, or cause cell abnormalities that resemble precancerous conditions. Thus, you may want to have a second Pap smear after your infection has been treated, but no sooner than one month after your first Pap smear.

Is the lab nearby?

Your doctor is likely to communicate more often with a lab that's nearby. If it's far away, it may be a high-volume, cut-rate lab that's prone to errors. Your doctor may make money by marking up the lab fee on your bill, and it could be you who pays the price—in more ways than one.

How Are Pap Smears Classified?

The results of a Pap smear are classified according to how much of the surface tissue of the cervix is affected and the degree of cell changes that exist.

Right now, many laboratories are in the process of updating and improving how they classify and describe Pap smears. (They are switching from the old Papanicolaou class 1–5 system, which simply rates a cell from "normal" to invasive cancer, to the new, more descriptive Bethesda method, which includes an array of classification categories.) In the meantime, doctors have to sift through a hodgepodge of terminology.

It's important that your gynecologist use a lab that provides a full descriptive report, and that she understand the report and can tell you exactly what the report means. Being told only that your Pap smear is "precancerous" or "possibly precancerous" or even just "abnormal" isn't good enough. Don't let ominous-sounding terms stop you from asking questions. In most cases these words *don't* mean cancer, although they may indicate cell changes that could eventually lead to cancer. Keep in mind that many hysterectomies are performed for "suspected cancer"; yet the removed uterus shows no signs of cancer. Don't be frightened into an operation you don't need.

All cytopathologists (experts in the study of diseased cells) use one of three, or a mix of three, classification systems that provide a continuum from normal to cancerous. To describe cell changes, they may use the term *dysplasia,* which means "abnormal development of cells" that may or may not be cancerous, or *cervical intraepithelial neoplasm* (CIN), which means, simply, "new and abnormal tissue growth" that may or may not be cancerous "among the cells lining the cervix." They may also use a newer term, *squamous* (a flat surface cell) *intraepithelial lesion* (SIL), part of the Bethesda classification method. Using these terms, they rate a smear as exhibiting mild, moderate, or severe dysplasia; CIN I, II, or III; low- or high-grade SIL; or invasive cancer.

Find out exactly how your Pap smear was graded. It will help you decide if the treatment your doctor recommends is appropriate. You may also want to request a copy of the pathologist's report. You can always have a second pathologist read your Pap smear, too, if the report seems ambiguous or incomplete.

——————— *What You Need to Know If Your Pap Smear Is Abnormal*

- If your Pap smear falls into the "abnormal but benign" category (the old Class 2 Pap), find out exactly what this means. Do you have a bacterial or fungal infection? Inflammation associated with the use of an IUD or exposure to DES? Cell changes that would indicate a viral infection such as herpes or venereal warts? Your lab report should include this information.

If it's an infection, your doctor will "treat and repeat." He'll give you medication for the condition and take another Pap smear in about three months. (Wait at least a month to have a second Pap smear, because it takes time for cervical cells to regrow, and a second smear taken too soon after the first may miss abnormalities.)

If your second Pap smear is abnormal, your doctor may be willing to "treat and repeat" again. Or he may want to do further diagnosis, as he would for a suspicious Pap smear, although many doctors would contend that this is unnecessary.

- If your Pap smear is "clearly abnormal," again find out exactly what this means. If you have mild dysplasia (CIN I, or a low-grade squamous intraepithelial lesion), keep in mind that this condition is of "indeterminate neoplastic potential." That is, it may or may not go on to become cancerous, and it never leads directly to cancer without going through other stages first. Up to 40 percent of cases of mild dysplasia disappear without treatment. (They are more likely to regress after a biopsy, even when it is unlikely that all the abnormal cells have been removed during the biopsy. Doctors do not know why this sometimes occurs.)

  Some doctors do not treat mild dysplasia, at least not immediately. They keep tabs on it with Pap smears every three months or so. Others will want to do further diagnosis, such as a cervical biopsy.

  How will your doctor decide if you need treatment? If he is aggressive, he may want to do further diagnosis (such as a colposcopy-directed cervical biopsy, see p. 103) and treatment immediately. If he is conservative, he may simply watch and wait for a time. Your risk factors for cervical cancer and your willingness to return for follow-up Pap smears may influence his recommended course of action.

  Some doctors feel it is important to treat even mild dysplasia if a Pap smear indicates exposure to the human papilloma virus (HPV). This virus causes venereal warts, some too tiny to be seen. Some forms of the virus carry an increased risk of cancer. And since the virus is transmitted through sexual intercourse, being treated helps stop the spread. Women seem to develop immunity to the disease, so that after treatment they are unlikely to be reinfected by their mates. Their mates, though, can spread the virus to other women. (Men can be treated with little discomfort with a cream that peels the upper layers of skin off their penis.)

- If your Pap smear is "suspicious" (moderate or severe dysplasia; CIN II or III; high-grade squamous intraepithelial lesions; or carcinoma in situ—cancer that has not yet started to spread), you have a condition that most doctors believe has a good chance of progressing to invasive cancer unless it is treated. It's true that a few of these cases regress without treatment. The catch, though, is that there's no way for your doctor to identify those lesions.

- Of course, if your Pap smear indicates invasive cancer, you'll want to take quick action. But even invasive cancer may not mean you need a hysterectomy (see p. 104).

What Is Involved in Diagnosis and Treatment?

These days, most doctors follow a clearly abnormal or suspicious Pap smear with a cervical biopsy. They remove bits of tissue from the cervix, using a magnifying instrument called a colposcope that allows the doctor to view the lesions that need to be sampled. (Don't agree to a "blind" or random biopsy—one that's not directed by a magnified view of the cervix. Their inaccuracy makes them worthless.)

A biopsy can take from five to twenty minutes. Since the cervix has few nerve endings, the procedure causes little pain and is done without anesthesia. During the biopsy, bits of tissue about the size of half a grain of rice are removed, using an instrument that resembles a paper punch.

During the colposcopy, your gynecologist should also scrape cells from the cervical canal, a procedure known as endocervical curettage. The biopsy and curettage tissue samples are sent to a pathologist for microscopic examination. Both colposcopic-directed biopsy and endocervical curettage

103

are considered to be highly accurate ways of diagnosing cervical cancer.

If your biopsy confirms cell changes that you and your doctor decide require treatment, you may have several choices.

Most forms of dysplasia on the surface of the cervix are removed in a simple, in-office procedure that usually requires no anesthesia. The lesions are destroyed by freezing in a procedure called cryosurgery or vaporized with a carbon dioxide laser. Or you may be given a vaginal cream that sloughs off the surface cells of your cervix. Some doctors burn lesions with a cauterizing probe, but because this older treatment can hurt and is more likely to cause the cervical canal to constrict with scar tissue, it's less frequently used nowadays.

Laser surgery is slightly more likely to destroy all the lesions in one treatment. About 5 percent of women who have cryosurgery, and 2 percent who have laser surgery, will need a second treatment to be cured.

If your abnormal cells extend into the cervical canal, your doctor may suggest a cone biopsy (or conization), a surgical procedure in which a cone-shaped piece of tissue is removed from the center of the cervix. Conization should *not* be done prior to obtaining the pathologist's report on your colposcopic biopsy and endocervical curettage. Because it is surgery and involves general anesthesia and a hospital stay, conization is usually reserved for cases in which invasive cancer needs to be ruled out.

If your doctor says you need a conization, make sure you understand exactly why he thinks this is the best treatment for your condition. If you aren't satisfied that this treatment is necessary, or if you think that lesser treatment might work just as well, get a second, independent opinion.

Cone biopsies can interfere with a woman's fertility and with her ability to carry a child to term. You can undergo more than one conization, but most doctors don't like to do more than two. (They'll recommend a hysterectomy instead.) If you do have a "cone," you should be followed closely in the future so that if abnormal cells return, they are detected early enough to be removed by cryosurgery or laser.

In select cases, conization can be used instead of hysterectomy as a treatment for very early invasive ("microinvasive") cancer. To be eligible for this treatment:

- Your cancer should not have penetrated more than three millimeters into the tissue of the uterus. (Some doctors will do conizations up to five millimeters' penetration, but this carries more risk that the cancer has spread.)
- The cone should remove all the cancer, not just part of it.
- The edges of the cone should show that the cancer has not spread into the blood vessels.

Simple hysterectomy is still the treatment of choice for microinvasive cancer. This is because even though a fairly large number of women have been treated by conization for this condition, no large, long-term study has followed them to see if the procedure really does cure their cancer.

Are you better off seeing a gynecology specialist for any of these procedures? The specialists, of course, say "Yes!" The general gynecologists say they can do many different procedures. The truth is that almost every doctor tends to specialize, doing some things well and other things not as well. If your doctor is honest with you, he'll hand you off if it's in your best interest. But it's up to you, the medical consumer, to choose the doctor who will treat you for a particular condition. There are no national figures showing how many conizations or colposcopies the average gynecologist performs in, say, a month. But these are questions you should ask your doctor.

You should certainly see a gynecological oncologist (specializing in cancer) for conization for invasive cancer. You may also want to see this specialist for any kind of conization; she does more "cones" than a general gynecologist, and her skill means she will be able to remove the smallest amount of tissue required, which means less damage to the cervix.

Colposcopy and colposcopy-directed biopsy also take some expertise; a doctor who's not highly skilled can miss lesions or take much longer to do this procedure. Here, as always, it's a good idea to ask your doctor how many of the procedures she performs each week, how long she's been doing it, how she was trained. If you're uneasy about your doctor's skill in any particular procedure, find another doctor. You may want to call the head of your local hospital's gynecology department. Ask her what doctor she recommends for your procedure, and why—is it because this doctor is the best, or because he's the only doctor in town performing the procedure?

——— *Hysterectomy*

At some point in her life, just about every woman can expect to be told she needs a hysterectomy, or at least that among her options for treatment, hysterectomy is the easiest and best chance for a cure. It comes out of a deeply ingrained belief among many doctors that, after childbearing, a woman's uterus and ovaries are disposable.

Your doctor may say, or imply, that a hysterectomy is "indicated" or standard medical practice, but this doesn't mean it's your best choice. So you'll want to ask . . .

——— *Do I Really Need a Hysterectomy?*

This is a crucial question. You'll want to explore the answer thoroughly before you decide whether or not a hysterectomy (removal of the uterus) is going to improve *your* quality of life. It's a question that should never be answered solely by your gynecologist (since she's the one recommending the hysterectomy). And your second opinion shouldn't come from her buddy-colleague across town.

Why should you doubt your need for a hysterectomy? Because despite increasing publicity about the abuse of this surgical procedure, and a drop in the number performed, there is good evidence that many unnecessary hysterectomies are still being done each year in the United States. Hysterectomy remains the second most frequently performed surgery, with 650,000 to 675,000 performed annually. That's *double* the rates of England and many European countries.

This wouldn't be so bad if U.S. women were receiving *better* health care. But that apparently is not the case. If anything, the facts suggest that women continue to be frightened or finagled into surgery they don't need. The most recent figures

How Often Should I Have a Pap Smear?

That's a good question. For years, the American Cancer Society recommended that every woman have an annual Pap smear. Then, in 1980, it began recommending Pap smears every three years, after two consecutive negative test results. The recommendation for longer screening periods was based on the concept that cervical cancer usually takes many years to progress from a precancerous dysplasia to carcinoma in situ to invasive cancer.

In 1988, however, the American Cancer Society adopted a policy similar to that endorsed by the American College of Obstetrics and Gynecology, the National Cancer Institute, and the American Medical Association. The policy states: "All women who are or have been sexually active, or have reached age eighteen, should have an annual Pap test and pelvic examination. After a woman has had three or more consecutive, satisfactory, normal annual examinations, the Pap test may be performed less frequently at the discretion of her physician."

What's a good time interval? A recent study by researchers at the University of Washington, Seattle, suggests that going more than two years without a Pap smear increases your risk of developing cervical cancer.

In this study, the risk for squamous cell cervical cancer, the most common type, was almost four times higher for women who had Pap tests every three years compared with women who had the test every year. Women who had the test every two years and women who had the test annually had the same risk. And women who hadn't had a Pap test in ten years or more had over twelve times the risk.

Besides the frequency of Pap smears, two other risk factors stood out. Women who had multiple lifetime sex partners or who were younger than age eighteen at first sexual intercourse were more likely than women without these risk factors to develop cervical cancer. Such women would be wise to have annual Pap smears, the researchers say.

You're Seldom Too Old for a Pap Smear

The women most likely to develop cervical cancer—those age sixty or older—are also least likely to have regular Pap smears, according to a survey from the Centers for Disease Control. Only 52 percent of women age sixty or older had had a Pap smear the previous year, compared with 81 percent of women ages eighteen to thirty-nine and 67 percent of women ages forty to fifty-nine.

Studies suggest that every woman benefits from having at least one Pap smear during her lifetime, no matter what her age. This is because cervical cancer is two to three times more likely to be found in pre-viously unscreened women over age sixty-five than in women age sixty-five or younger.

Women who have had regular Pap smears during their younger years should have at least two con-secutive negative Pap smears be-tween ages sixty and seventy, with the option to stop screening at age seventy, says the American Geria-trics Society. They base their rec-ommendation on a study from Swe-den that shows that the incidence of cervical cancer is low enough in women age seventy or older who have had at least one normal Pap smear in the previous ten years to recommend discontinuing screen-ing at age seventy.

from the National Centers for Health Statistics (1987) show that only 11 percent of hysterectomies were performed for can-cer, one of the few situations in which the operation is lifesav-ing. The overwhelming majority were performed for conditions that might have been treated by other means.

Statistics also show wide regional variations in the number of hysterectomies performed per one thousand women, which experts say means the operation is being performed too often in some regions. Rates almost double (to eight per one thou-sand) in the South. And they shoot up when communities have a surplus of hospital beds and doctors.

Why do gynecologists perform unnecessary hysterecto-mies? No one knows for sure. Some doctors truly believe the operation is in the patient's best interest, even though they'll

Why Should I Think Twice About Having a Hysterectomy?

● Hysterectomy carries a high risk of postoperative depression and other hormone-related psychological problems, especially in women who have the surgery for other than life-threatening illness.

● It can put a serious crimp in your sexual desire and your ability to achieve orgasm.

● It can cause urinary tract, bowel, and back and joint problems.

● It is major surgery with a risk of death of 1–2 per 1,000 operations performed.

● One-quarter to one-half of women have complications of fever or hemorrhage following the operation.

admit it's a "judgment call" with which others may disagree. Some doctors are still waiting for "proof" that the operation has adverse effects. They can find fault with virtually every one of the many studies in medical literature detailing its harms. They blame the postsurgical problems they see on prior psychological imbalances, not on the operation.

The hard truth may also be that greed plays a part in your doctor's recommendation that you have your uterus removed. Hysterectomies are more lucrative than medical management of a chronic gynecological problem. And they're a lot easier to do than some of the alternative surgical techniques used to avoid hysterectomy. Since your doctor can probably perform a hysterectomy himself, but perhaps not the more specialized (and complicated) surgical alternatives, he may suggest a hysterectomy as your best option to avoid losing you as a bill-paying patient.

And why do women agree to unnecessary hysterectomies, even ask for them?

They fall into the trap of getting one-sided information from their doctor. They let an unwarranted fear of cancer drive them to make hasty decisions. They may have never been treated appropriately for their pain or other physical symptoms, so they see no alternative. They believe a hysterectomy will cure their symptoms, when, in fact, they may simply be exchanging one set of symptoms for another.

So what does all this mean for someone whose uterus is on the line?

First, don't let the recommendation for a hysterectomy scare you. Remember, there are few cases where it's absolutely necessary. Second, even if you trust your doctor, don't rely on information from him alone to make your decision.

"In some ways, the situation has gotten worse," says Nora Coffey, founder and director of the HERS (Hysterectomy Educational Resources and Services) Foundation. "Gynecologists now understand that women are going to say, 'Well, I am not going to have a hysterectomy. I want to know all my options.' In response, they are getting awfully good at saying all the right things, and still, ending up with: 'But for *you*, dear, there just isn't any other choice.' " That's when it's up to you to determine your own options.

─────── **When Is a Hysterectomy Appropriate?**

The latest statistics show that hysterectomies are most likely to be performed for fibroid tumors, uterine prolapse, and endometriosis. This doesn't necessarily mean the operation is your best choice for any one of these conditions, though. All three can be treated by other means, although you'll do best to find a doctor specializing in your particular condition for treatments such as myomectomy for fibroids (p. 115), laser surgery for endometriosis (p. 117), and uterine resuspension for prolapse (p. 120). These treatments don't always provide a permanent cure, and they do have their own risks, which you'll need to weigh against the risks associated with hysterectomy.

Tell your doctor in no uncertain terms if you consider hysterectomy a last resort. Many gynecologists see hysterectomy as the treatment of choice, particularly for women age forty or older. You may want to ask your doctor if his recommendation is influenced by your age.

Hysterectomy definitely *is* necessary for invasive (spread-

In Case of Emergency . . .

These days, emergency hysterectomies are rarely necessary. Even in the case of ectopic pregnancy (where the fetus grows outside the uterus, usually in the fallopian tubes) or a ruptured abscess, uterus-preserving surgery is possible. It's only in the case of uncontrollable life-threatening bleeding, a rare problem most often associated with childbirth (but also seen with blood-clotting disorders and endometriosis), that a hysterectomy must be performed immediately to save a woman's life.

You are more likely to require emergency abdominal surgery if you have had pelvic inflammatory disease, endometriosis, or a history of cystic ovaries. But in most of these cases, you will have at least two or three hours to have a meaningful discussion with your doctor regarding your options and risks. If you want this information in writing as well, your doctor should be prepared to outline the salient features of what he has discussed with you. It's *his* responsibility as well as yours to make sure you understand what the operation may entail.

It's "absolutely appropriate" to tell your doctor that you don't want a hysterectomy unless it is necessary to save your life, says Dwayne Hull, M.D., a doctor whose business, Physician's Risk Control, helps doctors develop patient consent forms and procedures. If you want, add this request to your surgical consent form and have the doctor note it on your medical record. (See Chapter 6, "Keeping a Record.")

Plan ahead. Tell your regular gynecologist about your wishes: he may perform the surgery, or at least troubleshoot for you at the hospital. Tell your husband. In an emergency, it may be he who signs the consent forms. "Does a woman who is in pain and distress just acquiesce to the surgeon's first suggestion? Women need to become informed of their options *before* they get into an intractable situation," Dr. Hull says.

ing) cancer of the uterus, vagina, fallopian tubes, and ovaries, and usually also for invasive cervical cancer; for severe uncontrollable infection (usually associated with pelvic inflammatory disease); for severe, uncontrollable bleeding; for life-threatening blockages of the bladder or bowels by the uterus or growths on the uterus; and for some rare complications of childbirth, such as uterine rupture.

━━━━━ **What Kind of Hysterectomy Do I Need?**

There are several different kinds of hysterectomies and related operations. You'll want your doctor to make clear exactly which organs are being removed, which aren't, and which, if any, are up for grabs. You may want to note this in writing, or add it to a surgical consent form.

- A *simple hysterectomy* removes the entire uterus with the cervix and the fallopian tubes. This is also referred to as a total hysterectomy. (It does not involve removal of the ovaries.)

- A *subtotal or partial hysterectomy* involves amputation of the uterus above the cervix. The cervix remains in place. Fewer nerves are severed during this surgery, so the bladder, bowel, and sexual functions are less likely to be impaired. But it means you still run the risk of cervical cancer.

- *Oophorectomy* means removal of one ovary. *Bilateral oophorectomy* means removal of both ovaries.

- A *radical hysterectomy*, reserved for invasive cancer, involves removal of the uterus, removal of the upper one-third of the vagina, and a sampling of lymph nodes in the groin. (It does not necessarily include the ovaries.)

- A *modified or type II radical hysterectomy* is similar to a radical, but attempts to preserve enough nerve fibers to the bowel and bladder to maintain normal function. Ask your doctor about this procedure if he suggests a radical.

- An *abdominal hysterectomy* removes the uterus through an incision in the abdomen, most often a 6- to 8-inch cut just below the pubic hairline.

- A *vaginal* hysterectomy removes the uterus through an incision in the vagina. Although it may be cosmetically acceptable, studies show that this kind of surgery has a higher postoperative wound infection rate, and that 5 to 10 percent of women having vaginal hysterectomy require further surgery for complications.

───── *Can I Save My Ovaries?*

In about 40 percent of hysterectomies, the ovaries are also removed. The double standard in medicine is: "No ovary is good enough to leave in. No testicle is bad enough to take out." Doctors contend that the ovaries could become cancerous, and that ovarian cancer is a deadly and hard-to-diagnose disease. This is true, but it's also so rare that some researchers have calculated that only one in seven hundred women whose ovaries are removed would have gotten cancer.

If you're age forty or older, your doctor may try to persuade you that you don't "need" your ovaries anymore, and that hormone replacement therapy will restore your blood hormone levels. In fact, researchers now know that the ovaries continue to produce an array of hormones well past menopause. They also know that hormone replacement therapy is far from perfect (see p. 121). Even if your doctor agrees to spare your ovaries, there's a chance the ovaries will stop producing hormones, most likely because the surgery disrupts their blood supply. Some studies show this happens to more than one-third of women, and in up to one-half of women who have one ovary removed. This is another side effect, though, that gynecologists will claim is "unproven."

───── *Are Fibroids Ever a Reason to Have a Hysterectomy?*

If you have "fibroids," join the crowd. Half of women age fifty or older, and 20 percent of all women, have these benign uterine tumors. (And many have no symptoms. The tumors are found during a routine pelvic exam.) Fibroids are seldom life-threatening, can be treated by other means, and tend to regress at menopause, all good reasons to say "no" to recommendations for a hysterectomy for this condition. *Yet fibroids continue to be the number-one reason doctors perform hysterectomies*, accounting for almost one-third. Why is that?

- Women have been the victims of an arbitrary rule of thumb among gynecologists to monitor fibroids over a period of time, usually years, and then to recommend a hysterectomy if and

HERS: Hysterectomy Educational Resources and Services

Nora Coffey is a woman with a mission. Since her hysterectomy in 1978 and its devastating aftereffects, she has been helping other women avoid the same fate. Her organization, the Hysterectomy Educational Resources and Services (HERS) Foundation, offers phone counseling and a nationwide referral service to doctors knowledgeable in alternatives to hysterectomy. HERS also offers studies published in medical literature detailing the negative effects of hysterectomy and ovary removal. For information, write or call the HERS Foundation, 422 Bryn Mawr Avenue, Bala Cynwyd, Pennsylvania 19004 (1-215-667-7757).

Why a Fertility Surgeon May Be Your Best Bet for Any Kind of Gynecologic Surgery

Pelvic surgery can cause adhesions, tough sheets of scar tissue that encase and constrict organs. The result: pain, and in some cases, infertility.

Doctors who are fertility or reproductive surgeons are trained to operate in a way that minimizes adhesions and scarring. (In fact, they often do surgery to *remove* adhesions and scars caused by infections or a previous operation.) They use wetting solutions and techniques that limit blood loss. They use fine suture material and small instruments. They rinse out the area with warm saline to remove bits of tissue or blood, and they may cover denuded tissue with sheets of gelatinlike cellulose to prevent adhesions. Their gentler touch may prevent trouble down the line.

How can you find a reproductive surgeon? Asking the chief of your local hospital's obstetrics and gynecology department is a good start. Larger hospitals sometimes have departments of reproduction and endocrinology, and can refer you to a doctor on staff.

when fibroids have grown to the point where the uterus is the size of a twelve-week pregnancy (about three and a half inches in diameter). In fact, conservative gynecologists say *symptoms*, rather than size, are the best indicators that it's time to do something about fibroids. If you have heavy bleeding during your menstrual periods, pain, hyperplasia (overgrowth of the uterine lining), or pressure on your bladder or bowel, you may decide the risk of surgery is worth the benefits. If you have fibroids your doctor is "watching," you should ask:

- How many fibroids do I have? (They tend to occur in clusters.)
- How big are they?
- Where on my uterus are they located? (They can be on the outside, inside, or in the wall of the uterus.)
- How fast are they growing?
- Do you plan to recommend a hysterectomy in the future?

Your doctor may need to do ultrasound or laparoscopy to give you some of these answers.

- Women are not being offered alternatives to hysterectomy. Even though surgery to remove fibroids without removing the uterus ("myomectomy") is popular in Europe, many U.S. doctors are reluctant to perform this operation, especially on women who have completed childbearing. Their reasons: myomectomy can be difficult and time-consuming surgery, with a higher complication rate than hysterectomy. Studies show that it may involve extensive blood loss, the formation of painful scar tissue, a longer hospital stay, and more postoperative pain than hysterectomy. This is why it's so important to find a skilled surgeon who can minimize those complications, says Lynn Payer, author of *How to Avoid a Hysterectomy* (Pantheon Books, New York, 1987).

  It's true that myomectomy can be long and complicated, especially for multiple tumors. But doctors skilled in the operation say a well-performed myomectomy involves no more risks or complications than hysterectomy. (Myomectomy can be done with laser surgery, which involves less bleeding. And fibroids inside the uterus can sometimes be removed through the vagina, with a telescopelike instrument called a hysteroscope.)

115

The fact is that most gynecologists simply can't do this kind of surgery, or at least can't do it well. They'll recommend what they know how to do—hysterectomies.

• Even when they *do* perform myomectomy, too many doctors do an incomplete job. They remove only the tumors on the surface of the uterus, leaving those within the uterine wall or those protruding into the uterine cavity to continue to grow and cause problems. They may even tell a woman her fibroids have "regrown," never admitting that they didn't remove them all. In fact, it can be difficult to remove every fibroid, since budding, or seedling, fibroids can be as small as a pea. The doctor's inability or unwillingness to remove all the fibroids, plus the tendency for new ones to grow, is why one in four women who have myomectomies go on to have additional surgery, usually a hysterectomy. (The recurrence rate is much lower for patients who have solitary tumors than for those with multiple tumors—27 percent versus 59 percent.)

Since they rely on estrogen to grow, fibroids are sometimes treated with one of the estrogen-blocking drugs also used to treat endometriosis—Danazol or Synarel. These drugs are most often used on a short-term basis to shrink fibroids prior to surgery or to relieve an older woman's symptoms until she reaches menopause, when fibroids tend to shrink naturally.

——— *Does Endometriosis Mean I Need a Hysterectomy?*

Gynecologists used to give the symptoms of endometriosis a different label: *husbanditis.* Women who experienced pain during sex or menstrual periods so excruciating they took to bed were simply rejecting their feminine role, doctors said. The solution: tranquilizers and painkillers, and if those didn't work, a hysterectomy.

These days, gynecologists get mixed reviews. Too many still assume a woman's symptoms are all in her head. According to a recent survey by the Endometriosis Association, a Milwaukee-based women's self-help group, 75 percent of women with endometriosis were told by a doctor that their pain was psychological, before endometriosis was diagnosed. And doctors who treat the disease say they see many patients who have had symptoms for ten to fifteen years and have seen numerous doctors before their condition is diagnosed.

When the condition finally is detected, blunders in treatment abound, according to reports to the Endometriosis Association. Doctors doing surgery for the condition may not even recognize some forms of the disease. And some may prescribe hormones in a way that makes symptoms worse. It's no wonder the number of hysterectomies performed for endometriosis has increased dramatically, with 20 percent now being performed for endometriosis despite impressive advances in alternative treatments. It's true that the disease is more often diagnosed these days, but for many women it's still not found early enough to prevent their symptoms from becoming debilitating.

In endometriosis, tissue that normally lines the uterus and bleeds every month in response to hormone stimulation migrates outside the uterus and attaches to other organs, usually the ovaries, bowel, and bladder. The result is intense pain, swelling, and webs of scar tissue that strangle organs.

A firm diagnosis of endometriosis can be made *only* by a surgical procedure that allows the doctor to view the internal organs, either

- laparoscopy, in which the doctor inserts a surgical viewing tube (a laparoscope) into a half-inch slit near the navel, or
- laparotomy, a much more serious operation in which the surgeon opens up the belly with an eight-inch incision.

Both procedures can also detect conditions with symptoms similar to endometriosis: pelvic inflammatory disease, ovarian cysts, appendicitis, ectopic pregnancy, even rare but deadly ovarian cancer.

With either method, endometrial implants can be removed by scalpel, cauterizing probe, or laser. State-of-the-art treatment—laseroscopy—uses the laparoscope to view the internal organs and a laser to vaporize endometrial implants. An even newer technique—videolaseroscopy—includes a video camera that magnifies the view of the belly and records the operation.

Drugs are also a treatment option. Both pregnancy and menopause cause endometrial implants to shrink, and the drugs used to treat endometriosis create pseudo-pregnancy or -menopause by counteracting the ovaries' hormone production (which stimulates endometrial growth).

Birth control pills, especially those with a high ratio of progesterone to estrogen, are used for mild cases in younger women, even though research suggests they worsen symptoms in some women.

In more severe cases, stronger drugs are prescribed. Danazol (Danocrine), based on a male hormone, shrinks endometrial implants but has serious side effects. It can cause weight gain, bloating, depression or irritability, muscle cramps, and masculinizing effects such as voice-deepening that in some cases are irreversible. Gonadotropin releasing hormone agonists (GnRH-a) are new drugs that also suppress hormone production but appear to have milder side effects than danazol. The first such drug on the market, Synarel, is sold as a nasal spray. (A total of four such drugs are available.)

Because of side effects, both drugs are most often used temporarily (danazol for no more than nine months, GnRH-a for no more than six months) to shrink implants prior to surgery or pregnancy, and sometimes after surgery.

Side effects, cost (both Danocrine and Synarel are very expensive), and the fact that endometriosis frequently returns soon after drugs are stopped are leading an increasing number of doctors to suggest surgery first, at the time of diagnosis.

If that's your choice, make sure you find a well-qualified doctor. One way to begin that process is through the Endometriosis Association, Box 92187, Milwaukee, Wisconsin 53202 (1-800-992-ENDO). This group will put you in touch with nearby members who may know doctors in your area who treat this disease.

If you are selecting a doctor to do laser surgery, be especially wary. Any doctor can buy a laser, set up shop as a "specialist," and practice on unwitting patients.

Camran Nezhat, M.D., the Endometriosis Association's adviser and a pioneer in the area of videolaseroscopy, suggests you ask these questions of a potential surgeon:

- How long have you been performing laseroscopy (or videolaseroscopy)?

- Have you treated only mild to moderate disease, or more extensive cases?

- On the average, how many cases do you do a week? (Dr. Nezhat says it takes at least one year of continuous practice of an average of two to three cases a week—a total of 150 cases—before a doctor is comfortable doing laser or videolaser surgery for endometriosis.)

The American Board of Obstetrics and Gynecology does not provide subcertification for laser surgery. Doctors doing laser surgery can join professional societies, such as the Gynecologic Laser Society or the American Association of Gynecologic Laparoscopists. These societies do not necessarily require that a doctor meet competency standards to become a member.

Even knowing their other options, some women do eventually decide on a hysterectomy, says Mary Lou Ballweg, founder of the Endometriosis Association. "Women have had marriages break up because of painful sex or infertility problems. Some have lost jobs, and health insurance, because their pain has kept them from working full-time. For some, hysterectomy is the way to get their lives back."

Doctors disagree on whether the ovaries need to be removed during hysterectomy for endometriosis. One study reports that about 85 percent of women with endometriosis severe enough to warrant a hysterectomy will have a recurrence of the disease if all ovarian tissue is not removed. But some doctors who use an intense drug regimen prior to surgery say they have few recurrences even when the ovaries are preserved.

And some doctors say it's vital to wait six to nine months after the hysterectomy to begin replacement hormone therapy, to give remaining endometrial implants time to shrink; other doctors claim they can begin hormone therapy immediately with no ill effects. An unknown number of women do have a flare-up of symptoms while taking replacement hormones, although usually their symptoms are not as bad as before the hysterectomy.

Some doctors consider it something of a scam for an infertile woman with *asymptomatic* endometriosis to be treated for the disease with surgery or drugs in an attempt to improve her chances of becoming pregnant. Studies are mixed on

119

whether or not treatment improves fertility rates. "Here again, the result may depend very much on the surgeon's skill," Dr. Nezhat says.

—— *Should Prolapsed Uterus Be Treated by Hysterectomy?*

A prolapsed ("fallen") uterus is the second most common reason doctors perform hysterectomies. That's a shame, because once the uterus is removed, other organs can shift. Unless the surgeon also tightens up sagging ligaments and muscles, a hysterectomy can lead to prolapse of the vagina (which caves in on itself) or of the bladder or bowel. These conditions are difficult to correct surgically.

A well-performed hysterectomy with repositioning of other organs *will* solve the problem of prolapse. But many cases can be corrected (at least in part) without a hysterectomy. The alternative surgery, "uterine resuspension," involves repositioning the uterus and any other organs that have fallen, shortening the stretched ligaments, and reinforcing the muscles and tough sheets of tissue called fascia, all which hold the uterus in place. It may also involve tightening the muscles around the vagina and rectum. Variations of "resuspension" surgery abound, as do forms of prolapse.

More than most kinds of gynecologic surgery, repair of prolapse is an operation that can be easily botched, which may be one reason many doctors do not enthusiastically endorse it.

"Women who consider this type of surgery should realize it is not an easier or less invasive operation than a hysterectomy," says Wulf Utian, M.D., director of obstetrics and gynecology at University McDonald Women's Hospital in Cleveland, Ohio. "It is major abdominal surgery, and includes risks of scar tissue formation, infection, and blood loss."

That's why, if your gynecologist says this procedure is not for you, your best bet is have your second opinion come from a doctor who is an expert in this sort of operation. And it's *always* best to have the surgery performed by a doctor you know does prolapse surgery frequently and can handle severe cases.

There's also debate about just how well this surgery works, even when done by an expert. Studies report that the uterus falls again in 10 to 20 percent of cases (usually not as far as the first time, though). But some doctors contend recurrence rates are higher, and that evidence supporting this type of surgery is poor. "In cases of severe prolapse, it usually looks quite good in the beginning, but it usually doesn't take very long before symptomatic prolapse will recur," Dr. Utian says. Prolapse is never life-threatening, although it can be unpleasant and uncomfortable. You may decide you want surgery when the benefit of relieving your symptoms of pressure, urinary incontinence, and pain start to outweigh the risks, inconvenience, and cost of surgery. It's worth trying some alternatives, though, before agreeing to surgery.

You may want to ask your gynecologist about using a *pessary*, a device similar to a diaphragm that helps hold the uterus in place. Pessaries come in many shapes and sizes, so it's up to you and your doctor to find the one that works best for you. (Only one type, the ring pessary, can be worn during sex.) These devices do need to be cleaned every few months to avoid irritation, and in most cases, they need to be removed every few months and replaced by your doctor. This is why some women find them too inconvenient to use for long. In severe prolapse, they can also fall out. Most doctors offer them only as a temporary solution to younger women, and as the only option for women too old and weak for surgery. Still, you may feel that the inconvenience beats major abdominal surgery.

Losing weight and taking replacement hormones (which help to thicken the vaginal walls and tone up pelvic muscles) sometimes reduce symptoms of prolapse enough to avoid surgery. Treating a chronic cough can help, too, since coughing puts pressure on the uterus. Kegel exercises (designed to tighten the muscles around the vagina and rectum) may help mild prolapse, but doctors say they are useless for more severe cases.

Hormone Replacement Therapy

One of the most mind-boggling health decisions a menopausal woman faces is whether to take supplemental hormones to replace those no longer being produced by her aging ovaries.

Hormone replacement therapy (HRT) includes estrogen, a

major female hormone that performs many functions, such as thickening the uterine lining. It often includes progesterone (usually a synthetic mix of progestins), a hormone that counterbalances estrogen, causing the uterine lining to shed each month as menstrual bleeding. And HRT occasionally includes androgens, male hormones that women, too, naturally produce in small amounts and that are thought to influence sex drive, energy levels, and mood.

Why is the decision so confusing?

- Because even among studies published in prestigious medical journals, findings are sometimes contradictory or hard to interpret, especially when it comes to the role of hormone replacement therapy in preventing heart disease or breast cancer. For example, several studies found benefits or at least no harm with HRT. But a few suggested increased risk for heart disease or breast cancer, at least for some women.

  Many questions about HRT remain unanswered, especially questions about the benefits and risks of long-term use of estrogen-progestin combinations. (Unfortunately, in the past, and especially with female hormone treatments, today's "medical miracle" has backfired to become tomorrow's horror story.)

- Because even doctors have trouble separating hype from fact, especially when it comes to estrogen's alleged ability to preserve youthful good looks and ensure a sense of well-being. As the National Women's Health Network points out in its booklet *Taking Hormones and Women's Health,* some doctors continue to claim that estrogen relieves depression and keeps skin "young-looking," even after a National Institutes of Health Conference in 1979 found no evidence of those effects. (For a copy of the booklet, send $5 to National Women's Health Network, 1325 G Street, N.W., Washington, D.C. 20005.)

  And drug companies are constantly marketing their various hormone replacement products—and funding research in this area—because it means big bucks.

  Despite the confusion, most gynecologists apparently think hormone replacement benefits outweigh the risks, especially for women who have had their ovaries removed. At a recent national conference on menopause, speakers' pro-hormone comments got rounds of applause from an audience consisting mostly of doctors, points out editor Mary Ann Napoli in *HealthFacts*, a newsletter published by the Center for Medical Consumers in New York City.

And more than four million women do choose to take hormones. Either they simply follow their doctor's recommendation, or, wisely, they get more information and decide that, for them, the benefits of HRT outweigh the risks, including those risks that are still unknown.

So how can you decide if HRT is for you? You can start by grilling your gynecologist.

Why do you think I should have HRT?

If you are bothered by hot flashes (upper body flushing usually followed by heavy sweating) or vaginal atrophy (thinning and dryness, which can cause painful intercourse), HRT definitely can help.

Estrogen *is* FDA-approved to treat both very uncomfortable symptoms of menopause. It controls hot flashes in about two weeks of use, provided the dose is adequate. Vaginal atrophy is resolved more slowly, depending on the severity of the condition. Without hormone treatment, hot flashes usually eventually lessen, but vaginal atrophy only gets worse. (If vaginal atrophy is a woman's only menopausal symptom, it is often treated with an estrogen-containing topical cream for as long as the woman remains sexually active.)

Although anecdotal evidence, and some studies, suggest that estrogen therapy can help other symptoms such as urinary incontinence, vaginal infections, muscle and joint pains, mood swings, and insomnia, it is *not* FDA-approved to treat these symptoms. "But women whose hot flashes disturb their sleep do sometimes find that estrogen helps relieve symptoms of anxiety or depression," says Isaac Schiff, M.D., chief of Vincent Memorial Gynecology Service at Massachusetts General Hospital. You may decide to try HRT to see if it relieves any of these symptoms, but keep in mind that you may need other, or additional, treatment.

Even if you aren't bothered by hot flashes, vaginal atrophy, or other symptoms, your gynecologist may recommend HRT. Her reasons? To help prevent osteoporosis (porous, fragile bones) and heart disease, the number-one killer of women after they reach the age of menopause. Admittedly, these seem like good reasons to take HRT, but is the evidence of benefits strong enough to subject yourself to the possible risks of prolonged hormone treatment? That's something you'll have to decide for yourself.

■ *Does HRT really prevent osteoporosis?*

Studies show clearly that one component of HRT, estrogen, can help slow the rapid bone loss that occurs after menopause. Some doctors think that even just a few years of hormone therapy will help prevent osteoporosis; others believe HRT must be long term. In fact, it's anyone's guess how long HRT must be given to avoid bone fractures. Treatment may well depend on the individual woman. It's also unclear what role progestins play in preventing osteoporosis.

■ *What is my risk for osteoporosis?*

Some doctors may frighten women by telling them just how widespread osteoporosis is among older women. One in every two postmenopausal women are "diagnosed" with osteoporosis. The truth is, though, that even experts don't agree on exactly how much bone mass a woman has to lose before she should be diagnosed as having osteoporosis. And ways of measuring bone loss are notoriously inaccurate.

What really counts is not osteoporosis itself, but what it can lead to—fractures, says Joseph Melton III, M.D., of the Mayo Clinic's department of medical statistics and epidemiology. "That's where you have real numbers and can come up with real risks."

According to his statistics, a white woman's lifetime risk of a hip or wrist fracture is about 15 percent; of a spinal fracture (fracture of a vertebrae), about 33 percent. (Most black women are heavier boned, and so are less likely to break bones as they age.)

Your own risks may be much greater than this, though, if you

- undergo menopause, including surgical menopause (removal of the ovaries) before age 45;

- are fair-skinned;
- are small-boned and thin;
- are inactive; or
- are a heavy drinker or smoker.

Why can't I just take calcium?

Researchers now know that extra calcium is useless in older women who are estrogen-deficient. Their bodies can't use calcium to build up bones unless estrogen is present. Women who do take estrogen, though, may reap additional bone-building benefits from a calcium-rich diet and regular exercise.

Does HRT really help prevent heart disease?

Evidence for this is less clear. It is known that one component of HRT, estrogen, raises blood levels of beneficial high-density lipoproteins (HDLs), a type of cholesterol that lowers the risk for heart disease. Naturally occurring estrogen may protect younger women from heart disease. After menopause, when estrogen levels drop, a woman's risk for heart disease climbs.

But there are also nagging suspicions about estrogen's role in blood clotting and strokes. Estrogen is generally not prescribed for women who have had thrombophlebitis (blood clots in the veins) or a stroke or who are heavy smokers. Most doctors, however, think that these negative effects are related to the dosage of estrogen. "Clotting problems have been seen in women who take birth control pills containing high dosages of estrogen. But they have not been seen in women taking postmenopausal estrogen, which contains much lower dosages," Dr. Schiff says.

Most studies do show that postmenopausal women who take estrogen (without progestins) are less likely to develop heart disease than are women who do not take estrogen. One often-cited study, done in 1985 by researchers at Harvard Medical School, showed that estrogen use cut in half the risk for both fatal and nonfatal heart attacks.

There is one major problem with at least some of these studies, contends Sadja Greenwood, M.D., author of *Meno-*

pause Naturally (Volcano Press, Volcano, Calif., 1989). "The studies ignore the fact that doctors tend to suggest estrogen to their healthier patients," she says, "and to discourage the use of hormones in women who already have risk factors such as obesity, high blood pressure, chest pains, diabetes, or heavy use of tobacco or alcohol." So it's possible that estrogen's beneficial effects are exaggerated in these studies.

"To get around this bias, what really needs to be done is a totally randomized study, where the women who get estrogen (and those who don't) are selected entirely by chance, not by a doctor," Dr. Schiff says. Such a study has yet to be done.

To make things even more confusing, researchers now think that progestins, the often-added second component of HRT, may negate at least some of estrogen's heart-protecting effects. Progestins are known to lower good HDLs and to raise bad LDLs (low-density lipoproteins) and triglycerides, fatty particles that tend to stick to blood vessel walls and block arteries.

Studies are yet to be done that look at the development of heart disease in women taking long-term estrogen-progestin combinations.

A National Institutes of Health study, the Postmenopausal Estrogen/Progesterone Intervention (PEPI), currently in progress, may help answer questions about the effects of estrogen-progestin combinations on the incidence of heart disease in postmenopausal women. Results won't be available for several years. Until then, it's up to you and your doctor to decide.

Heart disease is certainly more of a risk in women who undergo early menopause, either naturally or by having their ovaries removed. And many doctors do prescribe HRT for these women.

But doctors seem to be reluctant to prescribe HRT to women with other major risk factors for heart disease: obesity, smoking, high blood pressure, high cholesterol, or a history of blood clotting. "There is no evidence to show that HRT is harmful in these women," Dr. Schiff says. "Some of those doctors may not know the data; others fear that if their patient is at risk for heart disease, and gets into trouble, she will blame the hormones and sue the doctor."

One point on which all doctors agree: stopping smoking,

losing weight, exercising, and eating low-fat foods are surer ways than HRT to cut your risk for heart disease.

▬ What is known about the cancer risks of HRT?

Doctors say that women who decline to take replacement hormones often do so because of a fear of cancer. The unknown possible risks, perhaps, scare women most.

It's clear that estrogen, taken alone, in any form, increases a woman's risk of developing cancer of the endometrium (uterine lining) from four to fifteen times. Estrogen causes the uterine lining to grow and thicken, which eventually can lead to abnormal cell growth that can become cancerous.

That's why progestins are added during therapy. Progestin allows the uterine lining to break down and be shed as menstrual fluid. The monthly shedding prevents cancer from developing. Women who take progestins run less risk of endometrial cancer than women who take no replacement hormones.

One possible problem with this treatment is that doctors sometimes don't prescribe progestins for the number of days each month necessary to ensure complete shedding of the endometrial lining, which reduces the risk of endometrial cancer to zero. In the past, it was common practice to prescribe progestins for ten days. "Some doctors still do that, even though studies show that women need to be taking progestins twelve to fourteen days," warns Robert Rebar, M.D., professor of obstetrics and gynecology at the University of Cincinnati College of Medicine.

And many doctors don't prescribe progestins at all. "Currently, only about half of menopausal women taking estrogen also take progestins," Dr. Rebar says. Women who have had a hysterectomy may account for some of those; for them, estrogen alone is safe. Others are reluctant to continue to have periods, or develop premenstrual-like symptoms from progestins, and so their doctors don't include progestins or the women stop taking the hormone.

If your uterus is intact, and you are taking estrogens alone, in any form, you need to be monitored carefully for signs of endometrial hyperplasia (cell overgrowth), a condition that can lead to endometrial cancer. Some doctors do an annual endometrial biopsy, a quick office procedure that removes a bit of tissue from the uterine lining.

Problems with both cyclic estrogen-progestin therapy (given in staged doses during a month, resulting in monthly menstrual periods), and estrogen alone are leading an increasing number of doctors to experiment with a combination of continual estrogen-progestin therapy (given in the same dosage throughout the month). This may provide the benefits of both estrogen and progestins without monthly periods. The problem with this therapy, Dr. Utian admits, is that no one knows whether it creates a risk for endometrial cancer. "Most of us think the excess risk is eliminated, but that has not yet been proven," he says. (Most doctors do not do a yearly endometrial biopsy when using this therapy.) And no one knows its effect on blood lipids and heart disease.

The risks for breast cancer from HRT are much less clear. Most researchers agree that, theoretically, both estrogen and progestins could cause breast cancer, because they stimulate the growth of cells in the breast (and breast cancer can be induced by estrogen in laboratory animals). But most researchers think this effect is weak in older women, whose breast tissue cells are fairly inactive.

Most of the few studies done show no connection between hormone replacement therapy (mostly estrogen) and breast cancer.

But a recent study by Swedish researchers, published in the August 3, 1989, *New England Journal of Medicine,* did show a connection. Women who took replacement hormones had a 10 percent greater risk of developing breast cancer than women who had not taken hormones. That's a very slight risk.

Several higher-risk groups stood out: women who took estrogen for six years or more, and women who took more potent forms of estrogen not generally used in the United States.

More important to U.S. women, those who took estrogen-progesterone combinations for more than six years appeared to have 4.4 times the average risk of developing breast cancer. A major problem with this part of the study was that there were only ten women in this group, a number much too small to provide a statistically reliable result, according to experts reviewing the study for the *Harvard Medical School Newsletter*

(October 1989). Their consensus: the Swedish study highlights the need for more research, especially in the area of long-term estrogen/progestin therapy.

■ *What other risks does HRT have?*

Estrogen use has been associated with an increase in gallstones and gallbladder pain. Women who use replacement estrogen are more likely to have their gallbladder removed than are women who do not use estrogen. Obesity, high cholesterol, and diabetes are additional risk factors for gallbladder problems.

Replacement estrogen can cause flare-ups of some conditions that may have improved as you've gotten older. It can cause fibroid tumors or endometriosis implants to grow. It can also cause painful, lumpy breasts.

■ *Should I see an endocrinologist?*

An endocrinologist is a doctor specially trained in the treatment of hormonal disorders.

If your gynecologist's practice includes a large number of older women, and she stays up-to-date on the latest research, she may be the best doctor for you. If her practice includes many younger women and is mostly obstetrics, her focus may not be on the problems of older women. She may not be the best doctor to monitor your hormone replacement therapy. You may want to ask:

• What is your training in endocrinology?

• How many patients do you have on HRT?

• Why are they on HRT?

• How long do they stay on it?

• What kinds of problems do you see among them?

• Should I be seeing a gynecologist or endocrinologist specializing in this area?

Hormone replacement treatment can be complex. Various formulations and dosages abound, in pills, wafers dissolved

129

under the tongue, suppositories, vaginal creams, estrogen-releasing skin patches, even injections. Your doctor needs to know her way around this pharmaceutical maze in order to be able to prescribe what's best for you. Dosages given to women just beginning menopause, perhaps still menstruating irregularly, may be different from those given to older women who completed menopause years ago. Women with risk factors such as diabetes or cancer need to be monitored very closely. And different dosages may be needed depending on the symptoms being treated, or the side effects a woman experiences as a result of treatment. These are all good reasons to make sure you're seeing a doctor who knows what she is doing, whether it's your regular gynecologist or an endocrinologist.

■ *Do I have to decide now?*

Just because your doctor suggests hormone replacement therapy, don't think that you need to decide right now (unless you choose to do so because your symptoms are so distressing). There is time to wait and think, talk with friends, read up on the topic, even to see if your symptoms get worse or better. And don't think that deciding one way or the other about hormone replacement therapy leaves you stuck with your decision. You can always try HRT later if you want. If you decide you don't like the effects, or the bother, you can stop. And you can start again later if you find yourself being bothered by symptoms. A study by Sonja McKinlay, Ph.D., of the American Institutes for Research in Cambridge, Massachusetts, shows that many women do just that, with no apparent ill effects.

You may simply want to tell your gynecologist: "I need time to think about this."

■ *How long should I stay on HRT?*

The answer to this question depends on why you are taking HRT in the first place. If it's to relieve hot flashes or other temporary symptoms of menopause, your physician may keep you on it for several months, then gradually reduce your dosage. If your symptoms reappear, she may opt to continue the drugs for a few more months, then try reducing the dosage again.

If you are taking it to prevent osteoporosis or heart disease, it is likely that you will stay on it the rest of your life, or until side effects, inconvenience, or costs make you, in concert with your gynecologist, decide it is no longer worth the potential benefits.

Infertility

If you are slow in conceiving, you may do well to talk first with your gynecologist rather than an infertility specialist. Many gynecologists are capable of diagnosing and treating simple infertility problems, and may be able to save you a trip to an expert.

A gynecologist can provide direction that may help you conceive. For instance, he can help to pinpoint your most fertile time of month, or determine if lubricants or other products you or your husband use (including nonprescription drugs such as antihistamines and cough medicines) are thwarting Mother Nature. He should also recommend a semen analysis of your mate to make sure he is fertile. This is a simple, noninvasive test that checks the number, shape, and viability of the sperm.

A gynecologist usually also can perform some basic tests that will give him enough information to determine whether you need to see an infertility specialist. Before you agree to any course of action, make sure your gynecologist has adequate training and experience in infertility.

- How many couples has he treated, and for what?

- How many babies has he produced?

- If he suggests he can do a certain test or procedure, ask how many times he has done it, and his complication rate.

  Besides a routine pelvic exam, your regular gynecologist can probably do

- urine and blood tests to measure levels of various hormones;
- the postcoital test (examination of the woman's vagina and

The "Medicalization" of Menopause

If you decide to take hormone replacement therapy, you will (and should) be closely monitored by your doctor. This means yearly visits that include
- a full medical history;
- a full physical examination;
- questions about compliance (if you've been taking the hormones as prescribed, or if not, how you've been taking them);
- a breast examination by the doctor;
- a mammogram (breast X rays that can detect early cancer);
- a Pap smear (a sampling of cervical cells that is checked under a microscope for precancerous signs);
- a blood pressure check;
- blood tests to determine cholesterol and other blood fat levels;
- an endometrial biopsy if you are taking estrogen without progestins (and still have a uterus); and
- possibly an ultrasound examination of the ovaries.

This means that as long as you are taking HRT, you will be a patient. Some women may find that reassuring (and it's responsible—no doctor should give HRT without close follow-up). Other women dislike it, both personally and politically. They believe menopause is being treated as a disease rather than as part of the natural aging process.

Is menopause so bad? A recent study by Sonja McKinlay, Ph.D., of the American Institutes for Research in Cambridge, Massachusetts, compared women undergoing natural menopause with those undergoing surgically induced menopause (removal of the ovaries). She found significant differences between the two groups.

Asked to assess their overall health, the women undergoing surgically induced menopause were one and a half times more likely to report two or more chronic conditions such as arthritis, hypertension, diabetes, or allergic diseases. They were also the main consumers of medical services and prescription drugs. Twenty-five percent of the women undergoing surgically induced menopause used hormones, compared to 5 percent of the other menopausal women, and they used more tranquilizers and sleeping pills. Overall, they used medications at twice the rate of other women their age. They also reported 80 percent more surgery for benign breast disease than other women.

"In general, women who go through a natural menopause don't see it as a health problem. The majority go through it without going near a doctor," Dr. McKinlay says. "It's a relative minority who have symptoms severe enough that they see a health professional."

Getting Testy

Most women don't realize it, but their ovaries produce more than female hormones; they also produce male hormones (testosterone, or androgen—the two are basically the same). Women whose ovaries are removed, or who are past menopause, experience a large drop in blood androgen levels just as they do in estrogen levels.

Some doctors offer their post-hysterectomy and menopausal patients androgen replacement therapy. They are most likely to do this if a woman complains of lack of sexual interest or physical energy, or a general sense of depression, especially if estrogen therapy hasn't helped. (Some doctors, unfortunately, prescribe too-high doses of estrogen, tranquilizers, or other psychiatric drugs for these symptoms.)

Researchers at McGill University in Montreal have been offering androgen therapy for about twenty-five years, say Barbara Sherwin, Ph.D., and Murrie Gelfant, M.D., both of the department of obstetrics and gynecology at Sir Mortimer B. David–Jewish General Hospital and professors at McGill. "We noticed that when women whose ovaries were removed were given a combination of estrogen and androgen, they were healthier," Dr. Gelfant

notes. "They said they felt better; sexually, they said they functioned better; their mood was elevated. Even though they'd had their ovaries removed, they seemed perfectly normal."

Several randomized, placebo-controlled studies have confirmed these observations.

Androgen treatment has not been shown to increase a woman's risk for heart disease. Its two most common side effects—hair growth and enlargement of the clitoris—can be controlled by carefully regulating the dosage, Dr. Sherwin says. Side effects are fewer if the hormone is given by intramuscular injection every four to six weeks, rather than orally.

"This is *not* new therapy," Dr. Gelfant emphasizes. "The problem is that many gynecologists in the United States are just beginning to pick up on it. They often know nothing about it until they hear about it from their patients. We think that's terribly unfair to the women who could benefit from this."

If you'd like to find a gynecologist who offers such treatment, these doctors suggest that you contact the head of the department of obstetrics and gynecology at the nearest university hospital. Several estrogen-testosterone and testosterone-only drugs are FDA-approved for use for menopausal symptoms.

cervical mucus shortly after intercourse to determine whether the sperm are capable of penetrating the cervical mucus);

- a hysterosalpingogram (X-ray picture of the uterus, fallopian tubes, and ovaries to check for malformations and blockage); and

- an endometrial biopsy (extraction of a small piece of tissue from the uterus for examination to determine if a woman is ovulating).

If surgery is indicated, note this: although all board-certified gynecologists are trained to do certain types of gynecologic surgery, most are not trained specifically in surgery for infertility problems. Be especially wary if a gynecologist recommends an operation to open blocked fallopian tubes. These delicate organs can be further damaged by poorly done surgery, so you'll want to select a surgeon highly skilled in scar-minimizing microsurgery. That's most likely to be an infertility expert, usually a gynecologist who is board-certified in reproductive endocrinology.

When should you seek help for an infertility problem? If you've been trying unsuccessfully to conceive for a year or more (six months if you're age thirty-five or older), or if you've had pelvic inflammatory disease or painful periods (which could mean endometriosis), you may want to ask your gynecologist about possible infertility problems or see a board-certified reproductive endocrinologist. If their findings suggest that you may have difficulty getting pregnant, you may want to plan your pregnancies for when you are younger than age thirty-five and more fertile.

Studies show that, ultimately, a specific diagnosis for infertility can be made in all but 8 percent of couples, says Lori Andrews, author of *New Conceptions: A Consumer's Guide to the Newest Infertility Treatment* (St. Martin's Press, New York, 1984). Among women, the most commonly diagnosed causes of infertility are fallopian tube problems, 40 percent; ovulatory problems, 30 percent; endometriosis, 15 percent; and cervical problems, 5 percent. In men, they are varicoceles (varicose veins in the testicles), 39 percent; testicular failure, 14 percent; semen volume problems, 12 percent; endocrine problems, 9 percent; and tubal obstructions, 8 percent.

Studies report that success rates for reconstruction of fallopian tubes (extensive surgery to remove internal blockage and constricting scar tissue) is about 30 percent, Andrews says. The success rate for surgery to correct varicoceles is 40 to 60 percent.

Couples who are not able to conceive after surgery, induced ovulation, or other hormone treatments may move on to the next step: an "assisted" fertility procedure. This could include artificial insemination with the husband's sperm, or donor sperm, both fairly simple procedures with good success rates. Artificial insemination by the husband, in which the husband's sperm is injected into the uterus, has varying success rates, depending on the husband's sperm count; artificial insemination by a donor is successful 57 percent of the time per attempt, Andrews says.

Or couples may opt for in vitro fertilization (IVF), a process that allows fertilization to take place outside a woman's body and produces what the popular press has dubbed "test-tube babies." In this procedure, a woman is given hormones to induce ovulation, a process known as a stimulation cycle. Then, with a laparoscope, a number of eggs are removed from her ovaries, called a retrieval. The eggs are mixed with her husband's sperm, not in a test tube but in a flat, round dish. Once the fertilized eggs have started to grow (after the cell has divided about four times), a number of eggs are injected into the woman's uterus, where, if all goes well, at least one will implant and grow into a full-term baby.

Because there are few enough guarantees in this field of medicine, it's especially important to be careful in your selection of a fertility center or specialist.

"Although any doctor who wants to can attempt in vitro fertilization, it takes a special combination of expertise and talent to make the process actually work," Andrews says. "The average gynecologist or obstetrician—or even better than average fertility specialist—may try to provide IVF, but probably will not succeed."

According to a recent Federal Trade Commission (FTC) investigation, some of these centers have a reputation for inflating their success rates for "take-home babies." They do that by presenting their statistics in a way that is different from that recommended.

Clinics with lower rates will try to improve the appearance

of their program by telling you the number of deliveries per egg retrieval attempt, which ups their percentage of live births. But members of government are trying to standardize infertility centers' success rates by requiring that they be calculated by using live births per stimulation cycle.

The FTC investigation also found that even when success rates were calculated the same way, there was a wide range, from 1.5 percent (live births per egg recovery) to 25.5 percent.

The results of this survey and the clinics involved are available at government depository libraries around the country. Call your local library to find the depository library nearest you. Ask for "Consumer Protection Issues Involving IVF Clinics" (stock number 552-070-06387-1). This publication is also available for $31 from Superintendent of Documents, Congressional Sales Office, U.S. Government Printing Office, North Capitol and H Streets, N.W., Washington, D.C. 20401.

More than one hundred clinics also submit their yearly success rates for a variety of procedures to the American Fertility Society, which publishes them as a Registry Report in its journal, *Fertility and Sterility,* each January. This professional society also offers a number of booklets, including "Questions to Ask About a IVF/GIFT Program" and "Investigation of the Infertile Couple." For a list of their publications, write to the American Fertility Society, 1608 13th Avenue S., Birmingham, Alabama 35246 (1-205-933-8494).

Consumer information is also available from RESOLVE, a self-help group with chapters around the country that provide referrals, support, and information on infertility. Their address is RESOLVE, 5 Water Street, Arlington, Massachusetts 02174 (1-800-662-1016).

If you and your gynecologist determine that you should be seeing a specialist, choose carefully, just as you would any doctor who may be operating on you or recommending a course of treatment. If your gynecologist refers you to a particular doctor, make sure you know why she's recommending that doctor. If you shop for an infertility specialist yourself, make sure you have a get-acquainted visit and ask plenty of questions, including these listed below.

■ *Are you a board-certified reproductive
endocrinologist?*

Although it doesn't guarantee competency, board certification means that a doctor has met stringent training requirements and passed an exam given by the American Board of
Medical Specialties. Professional affiliations, such as membership or fellowship in the American Fertility Society or the Society for Reproductive Technology, do *not* mean that a doctor
has special credentials.

■ *What is your training in in vitro fertilization? When
and where were you trained? How many of these
procedures have you done?*

Do you want a doctor who has trained and studied for a
few weeks or a few years? Who just started doing the procedure
last week or five years ago? Who trained at a major medical
center with a nationwide reputation in infertility or at your
local hospital? Studies show that the greater number of a
procedure a doctor does, and the longer she does it, the better
she gets at it.

■ *What is your success rate for my type of fertility
problem?*

Doctors (and clinics) tend to specialize in the types of infertility problems they treat. Some are unable to handle certain
types of infertility, or won't take on many tough cases because
they lower the doctor's success rate.

■ *Do you have any restrictions on treatment?*

Some clinics require a couple to sign up in advance for a
certain number of "tries." Some allow only a certain number
of tries. Some won't handle certain kinds of fertility problems
or take women over a certain age. (These restrictions improve
their success rates.)

137

■■■ *How much is this going to cost us?*

Try to get a firm figure from the doctor, or, at least, a dollar amount per "try." Treatment for infertility problems is expensive, with the cost for in vitro fertilization at $7,000 or more per attempt. Always check with your medical insurance carrier to see what tests and procedures are covered before you have treatment. Many insurance companies do not provide coverage for in vitro fertilization.

────── **DES Daughters and Mothers**

Any woman born in the United States during the period 1941–1971, and even beyond, faces a special health risk. Her mother may have been one of the five million women who took the drug DES (diethylstilbestrol, a synthetic estrogen) during her pregnancy to prevent miscarriage. If this is the case, she runs a higher than normal risk for reproductive organ abnormalities, cervical and vaginal cell changes, and cancer. She also runs the risk of receiving inappropriate medical treatment, contends DES Action, a nonprofit consumer group that informs the public and professionals about the effects of DES.

Some doctors tend to dismiss women's concerns about DES, assuming that DES-related problems are pretty much a thing of the past, and that women age thirty or older are beyond the age when such problems are likely to occur.

Those assumptions can be deadly, says DES Action director Pat Cody. DES-related health problems are still emerging. It's true that the most serious consequence of DES exposure, deadly clear cell adenocarcinoma, is rare. It develops in less than one of every thousand DES daughters, most often in women ages fifteen to twenty-four, with a peak at age nineteen and a half.

And no one knows what possible cancer risks DES daughters face as they grow older, or if they use birth control pills or replacement estrogen. This is one reason DES Action suggests that DES daughters and mothers avoid such drugs. It is known that DES mothers have a 44 percent increased risk for breast cancer, so cancer screening is important.

138

Some doctors also mistakenly believe that a regular Pap smear and pelvic exam can detect DES-related problems. This is just not so. If your gynecologist offers what he calls a "DES exam," make sure it includes the following:

- A Pap smear not only of the cervix, but four additional smears (called a four-quadrant smear) from the vaginal walls surrounding the cervix. These smears help to determine if a biopsy (tissue sample) needs to be taken to check for clear cell cancer.
- Careful palpation (feeling) of the vaginal walls for any lumps or thickening.
- Use of an iodine stain to check the vagina and cervix for adenosis tissue, a glandular tissue not normally found in the vagina that can harbor clear cell cancer. (Regular tissue stains brown; adenosis tissue does not.)
- Some doctors also examine the cervix and vagina with a magnifying instrument (colposcope). This viewing device helps him detect and biopsy areas of tissue abnormality. "Blind" or unguided biopsies are less accurate than those done with the aid of a colposcope. If an area of abnormal cells is small, a blind biopsy may miss it entirely.

Paradoxically, some DES-related noncancerous conditions are *overtreated* by ignorant doctors. On a Pap smear, immature adenosis cells can be mistaken for dysplasia (abnormal cells) instead of what they really are, metaplasia (normal, fast-growing cells). This is why it's important that a Pap smear from a DES-exposed woman be labeled as such before it's sent to the laboratory for analysis. If there's any question about the laboratory report, you should request that the slide be examined by a pathologist familiar with DES cell changes.

Simple adenosis does not have to be treated; a woman whose doctor suggests this tissue be removed by freezing, burning, or surgery "to prevent cancer" should definitely get a second opinion from a DES specialist. (DES Action offers nationwide referrals to doctors specializing in the treatment of DES-exposed women. See the list of resources in the back of this book for their addresses.)

Be a DES Detective

What do you need to do to find out if you have been exposed to DES? First, ask your mother:

Did you take any drugs during the first five months of your pregnancy? (DES was given as pills, injections, and suppositories.)

If your mother says "yes," ask her why she took the drugs, and if she remembers the brand name. (DES Action has a list of the many brand names under which DES was marketed.) If she's uncertain, ask:

Did you have any problems during any pregnancy, such as bleeding, miscarriages, premature births, or diabetes?

If your mother did have any of these problems, there's more of a chance that she took DES, even if she can't remember.

If your mother's doctor is still practicing, DES Action suggests you ask him in writing for a copy of any records showing prenatal medication (and send along a self-addressed, stamped envelope). If the doctor is retired, the practice may have been taken over by another doctor who has the records. Your county medical society may know who has the doctor's records.

The information might also have been entered on your mother's hospital records at the time of your birth. DES Action suggests you write to the Medical Records De-partment of the hospital. Give your date of birth and your mother's name, and ask them to let you know what prenatal medicine is listed in your mother's record.

If your mother remembers the pharmacy she used, you can request copies of prescriptions filled for her during her pregnancy. Some pharmacies keep records going back many years; others do not.

If you suspect but are unable to prove that you have been exposed to DES, DES Action recommends you have the DES pelvic exam mentioned above that can detect physical signs of exposure. Besides adenosis tissue, distinct cervical abnormalities (a "collar" or "hood") are common signs. These are most apparent in women under age thirty. In women age thirty or older, the signs may have disappeared.

Unfortunately clear cell cancer may not be found on the initial DES exam; women who show no signs of cancer during their first exam may well develop it later.

Women who know they have been exposed to DES are advised to continue to have DES exams throughout their lives. Women who suspect but cannot determine if they have been exposed should have one DES exam. If the exam shows no signs of exposure, most doctors agree they can go back to normal Pap smears. Women with signs of DES exposure are advised to continue having DES exams.

When it comes to abortion, gynecologists don't necessarily practice what they preach. A survey by the American College of Obstetricians and Gynecologists shows that 84 percent of its members favor the availability of legal abortions. But only 34 percent perform abortions, and fewer than 2 percent do more than twenty-five abortions a month.

Fear of harassment or losing patients may stop some doctors. Others may have more personal reasons.

Perhaps one obstetrician-gynecologist is more honest than most when he says: "I deliver babies. I don't like to perform abortions and I don't think a woman who's having an abortion wants to sit in a waiting room full of pregnant women." That same doctor said he would gladly refer any patient who wants an abortion to another doctor or a clinic.

Some 87 percent of abortions are performed in freestanding outpatient medical facilities, such as family planning clinics or women's health centers. Ten percent are performed in hospitals or hospital outpatient centers. The remaining 3 to 5 percent are performed in physicians' offices. In all states but Vermont, the law requires an abortion be performed by a medical doctor, such as a gynecologist, family practitioner, or osteopath. In Vermont, abortions may be performed by a trained nurse-practitioner.

If safety records are an indication, this set-up works well. As with any kind of surgical procedure, practice makes perfect. It means the doctor or nurse-practitioner is performing the operation often enough to remain proficient, and the support staff know what to do when a problem arises. "Doing abortions at a clinic means you can schedule them sooner and perform them more efficiently and more safely than you would in a doctor's office," says Morton Lebow, a spokesman for the ACOG. Their statistics show that most doctors who perform abortions in their offices do four or fewer a month. At a clinic, a doctor could easily do that many in an hour.

There's no doubt that the safety record for abortion has improved since 1973, when abortion first became legal in the United States. Better-trained doctors, improved techniques, earlier abortions, and better management of complications such as infection have all helped make abortion safe.

Statistics show that a legal abortion, early in pregnancy, is seven times safer than carrying a pregnancy to term, and nearly twice as safe as a penicillin injection. The overall risk of dying from a legal abortion has dropped from 3.4 deaths per 100,000 abortions in 1973 to 0.4 per 100,000 in 1985—more than an eight-fold decrease. The few deaths that do occur are often a fatal reaction to the use of general anesthesia, which may be used at some facilities at the woman's request for mid-term or even early abortions. (Most abortions are done with a local anesthetic injected in the cervix, and sometimes with intravenous sedation. General anesthesia is never used for a late abortion.)

Women experience complications that require hospitalization in less than one-half of one percent of abortions. The most common complications are a perforated uterus, infection, or an incomplete abortion.

There's no doubt that the earlier an abortion is done, the safer it is.

Up to fourteen weeks of pregnancy, most abortions are done by a procedure called suction curettage, or vacuum aspiration. The woman lies on her back, legs in stirrups, on an examining table, just as she would for a gynecological exam. Her cervix is swabbed with a disinfectant, and, often a local anesthetic is injected around the cervix. The cervix is slowly dilated, then a suction tube about the diameter of a pencil is inserted. The tube is used to suck out the contents of the uterus, including the fetus and placenta. The entire procedure takes about ten minutes. Some women experience cramping during the procedure and for up to an hour afterwards.

Between approximately fourteen and twenty-four weeks of pregnancy, a technique known as dilation and evacuation (D&E) or dilation and curettage (D&C) is more often used. The cervix is dilated and the lining of the uterus is scraped with a sharp, spoonlike instrument, a curette. Suction is used to remove the contents, and forceps may be used to remove fetal parts too big to pass through the suction tube. This procedure can take up to thirty minutes, and is more likely to require sedation or general anesthesia.

After the twenty-fourth week of pregnancy, most abortions are done by the induction, or instillation, method. Less than 3 percent of all abortions in the United States are done this way. A prostaglandin or urea solution or a combination of both is injected through the abdomen into the fluid around the fetus. Uterine contractions soon start, and hours later the fetus and placenta are expelled. This method of abortion involves a hospital stay of a day or two.

If you're considering an abortion, you may want to ask your gynecologist if he recommends a particular clinic, and why. Does it have a particularly good safety record? Are there clinics he would avoid? Again, ask why. (See p. 52 for more information on outpatient services.) Or call Planned Parenthood, which has a phone listing in every major city in the United States. This nonprofit agency provides counseling and referrals for pregnancy and many other reproductive health concerns. If you are a minor, Planned Parenthood can tell you what your rights are in your particular state. Some states require parental consent, or a court waiver, before a young woman can have an abortion. The National Abortion Federation's toll-free hotline, 1-800-772-9100, can also answer your questions about abortion and put you in touch with NAF members in your area.

Breast Cancer and Fibrocystic Breast Condition (Mammograms)

Finding a lump in your breast can be terrifying. Even though it's likely to be a cyst (a fluid-filled cavity) or benign (noncancerous) tumor, there's always the chance it's cancer. You'll want to have the lump checked by a doctor as soon as possible. Take along a friend or your husband for moral support and as an extra set of ears. If you also tape-record your office visit, you'll be spared the stress of feeling you have to remember every word. You'll have an exact record of the conversation to review later.

Gynecologists, family doctors, and internists are all qualified to deal with the initial evaluation of breast lumps. Many women, especially younger women, are likely to see their gynecologist for this condition, since she may be their primary care doctor. But it's most important that you see someone you trust. During such times you'll be glad if you took the time to find a good gynecologist. (See "Choosing the Doctor," p. 2).

This doctor will feel the lump in your breast, detail your family history for breast cancer, and recommend the next steps. She may schedule diagnostic tests, such as a mammogram (breast X rays) or biopsy (removal of a piece of the lump for microscopic analysis). Unless she is a medical oncologist (cancer specialist), however, she won't be your primary doctor for the treatment of breast cancer. She'll refer you to a doctor (or group of doctors) specializing in the treatment of cancer.

You should know that most doctors today have dropped their wait-and-see attitude when it comes to breast lumps. Why? One reason is that, in the past few years, the number of malpractice suits filed against physicians for failing to diagnose cancer has shot up. Doctors are cautioned to check virtually every breast lump for cancer, even if it means ordering a large number of mammograms or biopsies for lumps that prove to be benign. Your doctor is likely to be calculating your odds for breast cancer (and her odds for a malpractice suit) every step of the way, and, as the person whose breast may be X-rayed, biopsied, or even removed, you will want to know those odds.

Should I Have a Mammogram?

That's debatable. If you can feel a suspicious lump in your breast, a *diagnostic* mammogram definitely is in order. If a *screening* mammogram is recommended to detect tiny lumps, you may want to think twice, depending on your age and your risk for breast cancer.

Mammograms are X rays of the breast that can detect lumps while they are still too small to be felt by hand. Because they can find cancer at an early stage, mammograms are considered to be lifesavers, at least for some women.

If you are between the ages fifty and sixty-five, the benefits seem to be clear. Studies done around the world show that regular screening mammograms can cut the death rate from breast cancer by 30 percent or more in these women. Few doctors dispute these findings.

But among women between the ages of forty and forty-nine or younger, the benefit of regular screening mammograms is much less clear, and the risk of undergoing unnecessary treatment (or not getting treatment you need) because of inaccurate results is much greater.

The American Cancer Society and the National Cancer Institute (along with nine other medical organizations, four of them professional radiology groups) endorse screening mammograms at one- or two-year intervals for women between the ages of forty and forty-nine. They base their recommendations primarily on the findings of two studies, as explained in the July 4, 1989, *Washington Post Health.*

One study, the Breast Cancer Detection Demonstration Project, was co-sponsored by the American Cancer Society and the National Cancer Institute. It enrolled 280,000 women between the ages of thirty-five and seventy to have mammographic screening for five years during the 1970s. The findings of the project suggested that, at eight years' follow-up, mammographic screening did contribute to longer survival rates for women thirty-five to forty-nine years old with breast cancer. This study has been criticized, however, for not including a control group (a similar group of women who did not get mammograms to compare with the group having mammograms). Instead, it used the general population as a comparison group.

The other study, the Health Insurance Plan of Greater New York, did have two distinct groups: women having mammograms and women not having mammograms. This study included some 28,000 women who were in their forties when the study began in 1963. After eighteen years of follow-up, this study found sixteen fewer deaths from breast cancer in those women who had mammograms than in those who did not. The problem with this finding, critics say, is that the difference in death rates between the two groups is not considered "statistically significant." That is, the difference is small enough to have occurred by chance.

To complicate matters further, more recent studies in Sweden and the Netherlands have found mammography screening beneficial only for women older than age fifty. And in some of these studies, a few women who had mammograms while in their forties were *more* likely to have died of breast cancer than those who did not have mammograms. This finding may be a statistical fluke; it may mean that younger women's breasts are more sensitive to radiation than older women's; or it may mean that breast cancer in younger women tends to be more aggressive so that, in some women, even early detection does not prevent death from breast cancer. Researchers still don't know the answers.

Two large professional groups, the American College of Surgeons and the American College of Physicians, have declined to recommend routine mammography screening for women forty to forty-nine years old. (They *do* recommend breast self-exam and a yearly exam by a doctor.) And a committee of cancer experts for the U.S. Department of Health and Human Services (which oversees the National Cancer Institute) recently issued its own recommendations. They say that the only women under age fifty for whom mammography screening may be wise are those with a family or personal history of the disease.

"We decided the potential benefit to women in this age group isn't strong enough to make general screening recommendations," says Steven Woolf, M.D., the task team's scientific adviser. "Even the most accurately done mammograms produce inaccurate results if you are dealing with someone whose risk is low enough, as it is in most women younger than age fifty."

So discuss the issues with your doctor before you agree to a mammogram. Chances are your gynecologist will recommend you have a baseline screening mammogram if you're thirty-five or older. If you're at risk for breast cancer because your mother or a sister developed breast cancer at a young age, you may be asked to have a mammogram as early as age twenty-five. You may also be asked to have a mammogram before you begin hormone replacement therapy, or if you're age thirty-five or older and about to begin taking oral contraceptives, to make sure the hormones aren't fueling a hidden tumor.

If you have lumpy breasts, as many women do, your gynecologist may recommend a mammogram to make sure cancer isn't hidden among the benign, fluid-filled cysts. She may also recommend a mammogram if you detect new lumps that don't fit the normal cyclical pattern of lumpy breasts (see p. 158). You and your doctor may decide a mammogram is appropriate in your case.

What Does a Mammogram Show?

Mammograms show the nature of a lump. If a lump is cancerous, its borders tend to be irregular or its shape poorly defined or spindle-shaped. A benign lump usually has well-defined, clear borders that are not irregular. Mammograms do not show cancer per se, so any positive mammogram needs to be confirmed by a biopsy, and many negative mammograms are also confirmed by biopsy. Screening mammograms that show a suspicious lump are usually followed up by a more extensive set of diagnostic mammograms before a biopsy is performed. (See page 206.)

What Is My Risk of Getting a False-Positive Result?

A false-positive result means that the mammogram detects a lump that, on biopsy, will prove to be nonmalignant, and you will have had an unnecessary breast biopsy. Unfortunately, the smaller a cancer, the more it may resemble a benign lump, so there is always a trade-off between finding early cancer and tolerating a certain number of benign biopsies. As mammography improves in its ability to detect even tiny specks, many doctors believe the number of biopsies done on nonmalignant lumps is increasing.

False-positive rates vary with a woman's age and with a doctor's diagnostic skill. It's been calculated that a woman who has yearly mammograms from age forty to fifty has a one-in-three chance of getting a false-positive result at some point during that time. A woman having yearly mammograms from age fifty-five to sixty-five has a 20 percent chance. And women younger than age forty have very high rates of false positives.

Ask your doctor his false-positive rate. But don't be surprised if he doesn't know it! Many doctors don't. There is no national average for false positives. Some breast cancer experts

147

say that finding two or three cancers for every ten biopsies is acceptable, and that that rate is achievable even at breast cancer centers detecting very small cancers. They say that any doctor who is finding one or fewer cancers for every ten biopsies he does is biopsying lumps he has no business biopsying.

──────── *What Is My Risk of Getting a False-Negative Result?*

A false-negative result means that the mammogram shows no signs of cancer when cancer actually is present. It can mean that you fail to continue to do breast self-exam, or discount lumps that do appear. It can lead to a delay in treatment. It's the reason the American College of Radiologists warns doctors not to rely on mammograms alone to make a diagnosis. They should be combined with a physical examination of the breast and a biopsy, if you and your doctor agree it's necessary to rule out the possibility of cancer, however remote.

Studies have shown that in 10 to 15 percent of cases of known breast cancer, the mammogram does not reveal it. In women under fifty, breast tissue is more dense, making it harder to detect abnormalities. For these women a mammogram is only 60 to 70 percent accurate in picking up a cancer. Mammograms are least likely to detect cancer in the dense breasts of young women who have never had children.

These days, virtually every doctor does a mammogram before she does a biopsy. The mammogram gives her information about the size, location, and possible spreading of the lump that allows her to do a more accurate biopsy. It may also reveal additional lumps.

In only a few cases can a mammogram clearly show a tumor that does not need to be biopsied. These include a tumor known as a calcified fibroadenoma and two kinds of fatty tumors, lipomas and fibroadenolipomas. Mammograms that indicate cysts can often be confirmed by ultrasound or needle aspiration (see p. 152) rather than by biopsy. Never hesitate to get a second opinion if your doctor recommends a biopsy you don't think you need. And if you are considering having a lumpectomy (see p. 157) if your lump proves to be cancer, tell your doctor that *before* your biopsy (see p. 153).

What Will Happen If I Don't Have a Mammogram?

Is your doctor willing to wait and watch for a month or so to see if the lump disappears on its own? She may, especially if you are a premenopausal woman with fibrocystic condition. But these days she may have you sign a release form that includes details of her findings and recommendations to you, and your refusal. It doesn't mean she won't still be your doctor. It means that, in a court of law, she won't be held responsible if your lump turns out to be cancer.

What Other Diagnostic Tests Are Available?

Ultrasound (which uses the echoes from sound waves to visualize lumps) can save you from having an unnecessary biopsy by clearly showing your lump to be a cyst. Ultrasound is 96 to 100 percent accurate at distinguishing fluid-filled cysts from solid tumors, making it better than either physical examination or mammography. It is most often used for small or deep lumps that cannot be felt by hand and are hard to pinpoint for needle aspiration. It's not a substitute for mammography, however, because it can miss small solid lumps.

Although the procedure itself is painless and noninvasive, ultrasound does require that you kneel over a tank with your breasts in water for up to thirty minutes, which may cause neck and back pain.

Both thermography (which supposedly shows tumors as "hot spots") and transillumination (shining a bright light through the tissue of the breast) are considered unreliable at detecting lumps.

How Do I Need to Prepare for This Test?

Ask your doctor to schedule your mammogram during the first week following your period, when your breasts are least tender. (During the X ray, they are briefly compressed.) Some breast screening centers also caution against wearing deodorant because some contain minerals that can show up on the X ray.

———— **What Is My Risk of Developing Breast Cancer from the Radiation of the X Ray?**

These days, most doctors agree that mammograms done at a reputable breast imaging center (see p. 151) are relatively safe. That is, your risk of developing breast cancer as a result of being exposed to the radiation needed to make the mammogram is minimal. (It has been calculated as comparable to the risk of getting lung cancer after smoking a quarter of a cigarette.)

Doctors do have some considerations, though. No one knows a woman's lifetime risk of developing cancer as a result of regular radiation exposure from yearly mammograms starting at age forty. It is thought that younger women's breasts are more sensitive to radiation exposure than older women's breasts, but no one really knows what that means in terms of an increased risk of radiation-induced cancer. (It has been estimated that about one in twenty-five thousand women who begin mammography screening at age forty will develop radiation-induced breast cancer sometime during her life.)

Studies have shown, too, that radiation dosages can vary widely among mammography centers, and among different kinds of breast X-ray techniques. This is why it's important to ask the radiology technician (who takes the X rays) what your radiation absorbed dose (rad) will be. Compare that figure with those below, which the National Council on Radiation Protection says provide good image quality at low dosage:

- For xeromammography (a technique where the image is produced as a positive, on paper), 0.8 rad per two-view exposure
- For film-screen with grid (a Venetian-blind type device that

improves image quality when X-raying large breasts), 0.8 rad per two-view exposure

- For film-screen without grid, 0.2 rad per two-view exposure

───── *Why This Place for My Mammogram?*

Your radiation risk and the accuracy of your diagnosis depend on the reliability of the mammography center's equipment and staff. The place you go for your mammogram should be able to produce sharp, accurate images with the lowest possible dose of radiation. It should employ radiology technicians and radiologists (doctors who "read" X rays and come up with a diagnosis) who are specially trained in mammography.

There's evidence to show that not all breast cancer screening centers are up to par, although they are apparently improving. In 1985 and 1988, the U.S. Food and Drug Administration did surveys to evaluate image quality at mammography centers around the country. Some three hundred centers were sent a model breast to X-ray. The breast contained seventeen test objects representing abnormalities commonly found in the breast.

In 1985, one-third of the centers failed the test. They detected fewer than eight of the "lumps" in the model breast. In 1988, 13 percent of centers failed (six more refused to take the test). The number of centers detecting ten or more of the test objects rose from 20 percent in 1985 to 44 percent in 1988. "It seems like most of the really bad centers have either improved or gotten out of the business," says FDA spokesman Fred Reuter. "We think there's still room for improvement."

Ask your doctor what criteria she used in selecting the mammography center. Does the center have X-ray technologists and radiologists who are specially trained and experienced in mammography? Does it use equipment specifically designed for mammography examinations? The American College of Radiology operates a rigorous accreditation program for mammography centers. Your local branch of the American Cancer Society or the National Cancer Institute (1-800-4-CANCER) can give you the name of the nearest ACR-accredited

151

center, or tell you if the center your doctor recommends is accredited. Mobile mammography "vans" are included.

——————— *Do I Need a Breast Biopsy?*

Your doctor has poked, pummeled, and X-rayed your breasts. Now he wants to do a biopsy—to remove some or all of the lump to examine under a microscope for signs of cancer. It may mean cutting into your breast. Should you agree to this test?

A biopsy is in order if your mammogram is suspicious (it shows signs of what might be cancer). Even when the mammogram shows no cancer, if the lump feels worrisome to the doctor he may want to do a biopsy. If you are over age forty and this is your first breast lump, if you're at high risk for breast cancer or have swollen lymph glands in your armpit area or nipple discharge, a biopsy is your best bet. If you're under age forty and your lump feels, acts, and looks like a cyst, you and your doctor may agree that a biopsy is not necessary at this time. Or you may opt for what's sometimes considered a kind of biopsy, fine-needle aspiration (see below).

——————— *What Kind of Biopsy Will Be Done?*

Your doctor may be able to do a biopsy without cutting into your breast. He can use a needle to draw out fluid and cells from the lump (fine-needle aspiration) or to punch holes into the lump and withdraw several cores of tissue (core-needle biopsy). He's more likely to do a needle aspiration or needle biopsy if the lump appears to be benign, is close to the surface of the skin, and can be felt by hand. It's also possible to do a needle biopsy on small lumps found deeper in the breast, but this requires more skill and special equipment to pinpoint the lump during the biopsy. Needle biopsy is relatively quick and painless. The doctor may first numb the skin where he'll insert the needle. It does not require general anesthesia.

Your doctor may want to do an "open" or excisional biopsy, making about a one-and-one-half-inch cut in the breast, then removing the entire lump, or, if it's large, a section of the lump. This kind of biopsy is easier than needle biopsy to do accurately. It's also the choice of women who want their lump removed even if it isn't cancer. Unless the lump is large or very deep in the breast, open breast biopsy is now generally done under local anesthesia on an outpatient basis.

Open biopsy does leave a scar. Although you can negotiate with your doctor as to where he'll cut (he can hide the scar under your breast or around your nipple), most doctors prefer to cut directly over the lump. They believe that if the lump does prove to be cancerous, a direct route makes it easier to see just where the tumor has spread. Some also think this approach is less likely to spread cancer cells to other areas of the breast.

If your mammogram shows possible cancer, and you intend to have a lumpectomy (see p. 157), if possible see a surgeon experienced in lumpectomy *before* your biopsy. He may be able to do a biopsy that is, in effect, a lumpectomy. He'll remove not just the lump, but an area of healthy tissue around the lump. It's harder for a surgeon to find and remove tissue that surrounded a since-removed tumor if the biopsy is not performed with lumpectomy in mind. If you intend to have a mastectomy, you'll most likely have what's called a two-step biopsy procedure. Your biopsy will be done first; if your tumor is cancerous, you'll return to the hospital within a few weeks for a mastectomy.

What Is the Biopsy Expected to Show?

The biopsy will determine, once and for all, whether the lump is cancer. A biopsy sample taken and read correctly is highly accurate. An open biopsy is slightly more accurate than a needle biopsy.

Who Will Do My Biopsy?

Your gynecologist usually won't do the biopsy herself, because it's unlikely that she's trained to do so. She will refer you to a team of cancer specialists. Surgeons are more familiar

153

"Medical Heretics" Versus the Medical Establishment

Do early detection and treatment of breast cancer actually save women's lives? Or do they only prolong the agony of a cancer death sentence?

The late Dr. Robert Mendelsohn and other "medical heretics" believed it was the type of cancer, not early detection and treatment, that determined how long a woman with breast cancer will live. They based their beliefs on the interpretations of the findings of a number of studies. And they pointed out that the death rate from breast cancer has remained the same for thirty-five years.

It's true that doctors used to believe, incorrectly, that all breast cancers remained confined to the breast until the tumor reached a certain size. Now they know this is not so. Some types of breast cancer grow slowly and rarely spread; others spread very early, and have sent cells throughout the body by the time they are detected in the breast.

For a woman with slow-growing cancer, early detection creates the risk that she will have a mastectomy for a tumor that would never have become life-threatening. And, as a statistic, it means she becomes someone who was "cured" by her cancer treatment, when in fact she might never have required treatment during her lifetime (she would have died of some other disease, or old age, before her breast cancer be-

came life-threatening).

For a woman whose cancer has spread by the time it's detected, early detection creates different risks. It means that she will live a longer time aware of her disease, probably have a longer treatment period that could mar her quality of life, and probably die anyway, in the time it takes for her particular type of cancer to run its course. In the meantime, she will appear to have lived longer than expected because her cancer was detected early. Her longer survival will make it appear that surgery and perhaps chemotherapy or radiation did help her.

Despite these possibilities, most doctors believe that early detection and treatment of breast cancer truly do have the potential to save lives— if not to cure, then at least to stave off the recurrence of cancer long enough to allow a woman to live out her life and die of something other than cancer. These doctors, too, base their beliefs on the interpretations of findings of a number of studies.

So who's right? Or, at least, what can we learn from this controversy to become better medical consumers?

First of all, it *is* true that the death rate from breast cancer has remained stubbornly the same for many years, with twenty-seven women per one hundred thousand dying of the disease each year. But this is not necessarily because of
(continued)

treatment failure. Doctors say it's because

• More women are now being diagnosed with breast cancer, probably because mammography screening is picking up more cases. This has kept the number of deaths from breast cancer constant, even though five- to ten-year survival rates have steadily, if modestly, improved.

• Regular mammography screening, the medical procedure shown in studies to be most helpful in preventing breast cancer deaths, is *not* widely used by the women who might benefit most. Less than 20 percent of women age fifty or older have regular mammograms. It won't be until many years after mammogram screening becomes standard that death rates from breast cancer will be affected. Many public health researchers believe that the biggest drop in deaths from breast cancer would come from making mammograms available to older, poorer women.

• The women currently dying from breast cancer include many whose disease was detected years ago, not by mammography but by clinical examination. Because their cancer was likely to be found at a later stage, their prognosis, as a group, is considered less favorable than that of many women currently being diagnosed at an earlier stage by mammography.

Doctors *do* have a lot more to learn about breast cancer. It's one of the most controversial areas of cancer treatment today. This is why being actively involved in decisions about your treatment is so important.

---

with open biopsies; pathologists, with needle biopsies. If you do opt for needle biopsy, experts say you should make sure it's done by someone who has done the procedure at least one hundred times. Ask. You don't want to be someone's target practice. Poorly done needle biopsies can mean an inaccurate diagnosis.

Do I Need Breast Surgery?

Your biopsy is positive: you have breast cancer. As scary as this is, and as quickly as you may want to act, there is no need to make hasty decisions or simply to do the first thing your doctor tells you, although you may later choose to do just that.

A four-week wait in which you decide on your medical oncologist or surgeon, type of surgery, and follow-up treatment won't hurt your chances for recovery. There is time for a second or even a third opinion. You may even find that another doctor doesn't think you need surgery. For certain kinds of breast cancer (such as lobular carcinoma in situ), doctors disagree on whether to operate or to keep close tabs on the condition.

────── *Which Doctor Should I See?*

If he hasn't already, your gynecologist will refer you to a team of doctors in your area who specialize in treating breast cancer. The team will include a surgeon, a pathologist, a medical oncologist (a doctor specializing in the treatment of cancer), a radiotherapist (a doctor who supervises radiation therapy), and others. The doctor most likely to oversee your care is a medical oncologist, especially if you need chemotherapy after surgery.

You want to make sure this team of doctors is the right one for you, selected because they use the latest and most effective cancer treatments, not because they play golf every Wednesday afternoon with your gynecologist. Ask your gynecologist:

- Why does he recommend this group?

- What kind of breast surgery are they most likely to recommend? (See p. 157.)

- Do they prefer chemotherapy or radiation?

- What other doctors would your gynecologist recommend, and why?

- Get the names of doctors who have treated your friends with breast cancer, then ask your gynecologist why he would or would not recommend any of those doctors.

You want to be assured that your gynecologist has given careful consideration to his referral. If you are not happy with his referral, get your own by contacting the nearest teaching hospital, medical school, or physician referral service at your local medical society.

Is your gynecologist going to stay involved in your care? Unless he's a cancer specialist himself, he's unlikely to be directly involved. If you'd like him to be available to help you sort things out, now is the time to ask.

What Kind of Surgery Do I Need, and Why?

Will your surgeon recommend a certain type of surgery based on your needs and preferences? Or will she recommend only the type she prefers to do? Before you say "yes" to any kind of breast surgery, know your surgeon's personal preferences, and your options.

Today, most breast cancer is found at an early stage, while it's still confined to the breast. This means that you may be able to choose one of two types of operations. You can have a "total" mastectomy, which removes the breast and may also remove some muscle and lymph nodes. Or you can have a lumpectomy (also called a segmental mastectomy), which removes only the lump plus a margin of surrounding tissue and is followed by radiation treatment of the breast. This kind of surgery is much less disfiguring than mastectomy.

A recent study, part of the National Cancer Institute's National Surgical Adjuvant Breast Project, showed that women with early stages of cancer do just as well with lumpectomy and radiation treatment as do women treated by having their entire breast removed. The study included more than eighteen hundred women with tumors that were about one and one-half inches or less in diameter. The women were randomly assigned to one of three treatment groups—total mastectomy, lumpectomy, or lumpectomy plus radiation. (Women whose cancer had spread to the lymph nodes were also given chemotherapy.)

The researchers found that lumpectomy, with or without radiation, produced results that were just as good as mastectomy. Eight years after their surgery, about 70 percent of the women in each group were still alive. The study also showed just how important radiation treatment is in preventing a re-

157

The Breast "Disease" That Is Normal—and When It Isn't

Many women's breasts become swollen, tender, and lumpy premenstrually, as hormones stimulate fluid buildup in the breast's milk glands and ducts. These lumps are usually symmetrical and appear in both breasts. They feel like masses of peas, grapes, or even golf balls. Doctors used to call this condition fibrocystic "disease," a misnomer because the condition is so common that it's considered normal. It's now called fibrocystic changes or condition.

When should you see a doctor about lumpy breasts? See her if you discover a solitary, dominant, or asymmetric lump or thickening, one that doesn't seem to fit the pattern of fibrocystic changes. (Regular breast self-exam will help you make this distinction.) In this case, you may need a mammogram, ultrasound, fine-needle aspiration (which will collapse the lump if it's a cyst), or a biopsy.

Most forms of fibrocystic condition are harmless. But two forms are thought to carry about five times the risk of developing breast cancer. They are atypical lobular hyperplasia and atypical ductal hyperplasia. (Both are an excessive growth of abnormal cells in the breast's glandular tissue.) Either of these abnormalities is found in 2 to 4 percent of the biopsies done on women with fibrocystic condition.

Only a biopsy can determine if you have either one of these forms. If you do, your doctor will follow you more closely than usual. She may want to see you every six months and do a yearly mammogram. She will do further biopsies only if you develop a solitary or dominant mass. Generally, hyperplastic masses are not removed. This is because hyperplasia tends to spread throughout the breast, through the network of milk ducts, making it impossible to remove completely unless the entire breast is removed. For women with a strong family history of early breast cancer (especially a mother or sister who had premenopausal cancer in both breasts), some doctors will suggest just that. But most doctors consider prophylactic mastectomy unnecessary, and in most cases, irresponsible.

If you have one of these high-risk forms of hyperplasia, with no family history of early breast cancer, your chances of developing breast cancer are still only one in five. These are pretty good odds. If your family history is grim, your odds may go as high as 50 percent.

Any diagnosis of a precancerous condition should be based on a biopsy, not a mammogram, family history, or "guessing." And keep in mind that even when a biopsy is done, not all doctors agree what cell changes are precancerous, or even cancerous.

currence of cancer in the breast. Among patients treated by lumpectomy, 40 percent who had surgery alone had a recurrence of cancer in the same breast within an eight-year period. Only 10 percent of those treated by both lumpectomy and radiation had a recurrence of cancer in the breast. Those women who had a recurrence were treated by mastectomy. These women have had the same rate of survival as women who did not have a recurrence. They were no more likely than the women who had had mastectomies to develop cancer that spread to the rest of the body. Their choice to save their breast did not put their lives at risk.

At many of the country's big cancer centers today, the majority of breast cancer operations are lumpectomies. But nationally, mastectomy is still the most common treatment for breast cancer. Why do doctors continue to do mastectomies?

First, not every woman is a good candidate for lumpectomy. A woman with a large tumor and small breasts, multiple tumors, or cancer that has spread to the skin, lymph nodes, or nipple will not have good cosmetic results with lumpectomy. Some women simply prefer a mastectomy. They don't want to have weeks of radiation therapy, nor to continue to check their breast for a recurrence of cancer, as *Consumer Reports* points out in its article "Is a Mastectomy Necessary?" (November 1988).

Some doctors won't recommend lumpectomy because they are waiting to see if the operation's long-term survival rates hold up. They believe there could be stray cancer cells in the breast independent of the tumor, and they would just as soon remove these cells by surgery, rather than depend on radiation to kill them. The ten-year survival rates of the women who have had lumpectomies do not support their fears.

What does all this mean for you? If you want to keep your breast, and your doctor says it must be removed, get a second, independent opinion from another doctor. And get a third if you need a tie-breaker.

By the way, the old, severely disfiguring breast surgery known as a radical (or Halsted) mastectomy is no longer recommended and is seldom performed. Even in the case of advanced cancer, radiation or chemotherapy usually shrinks the tumor enough to remove it with a modified radical mastectomy.

State-of-the-Art Cancer Treatment, Hometown-Style

Most women with breast cancer need not go to a big cancer center for the most up-to-date treatment. They can get the same treatment at a local hospital, thanks to the National Cancer Institute's Physician Data Query (PDQ) service. This computerized service allows any doctor or patient quick access to information on the most effective cancer treatments available.

To use the service, you need to know the exact type and stage of your cancer. Dial 1-800-4-CANCER, and ask for the PDQ State-of-the-Art Cancer Treatment Information for your type and stage of cancer. You'll receive eight to ten pages of information that includes descriptions of the different types and stages of your cancer, survival rates and standard treatments for each, and a list of current clinical trials in progress (studies that test standard treatments against experimental treatments).

Ask your doctor if he uses this service. Not all do. If he doesn't, find out why. You may agree to some sort of alternative cancer therapy, but you should know how it varies from that prescribed by the National Cancer Institute, and how effective it is compared to the National Cancer Institute's recommended treatment. (Cuts in recommended chemotherapy or radiation treatments are the most common variations, usually due to side effects.)

Some cancer experts say that women whose breast cancer has spread *should* go to a major cancer center, where doctors are treating many women with breast cancer every day.

What Kind of Follow-up Care Will I Need?

The results of your biopsy will give your doctor an idea of the follow-up care you will need. But this treatment won't be finalized until after your surgery.

If you have a lumpectomy, you will almost certainly be given follow-up radiation treatment, which is designed to kill any cancer cells that may remain in the breast. While some women who have a lumpectomy do well with surgery alone, right now there is no way to predict who they might be. Tumor size and

Breast Self-Exam Versus Doctors' Exams

Four out of five cancerous breast tumors are found by women who feel a lump in their breast. (That's because most women still don't have regular mammograms.) Many times, these lumps are detected by accident, perhaps while a woman is bathing or shaving her underarms. (That's because most women don't examine their breasts regularly for lumps. See page 206.)

Lumps found in this haphazard way tend to be large—one and one-half inches in diameter. Women who do occasional breast self-exam can find lumps that are about one inch in diameter. Women doing regular breast self-exams on average find lumps that are about one-half inch in diameter.

This still leaves room for improvement. Studies show that women can be trained to be able to detect lumps as small as one-eighth to one-quarter inch, although not all women can detect lumps that small.

Why should you examine your breasts for lumps when you can have a yearly mammogram or have your doctor check your breasts for you?

For one thing, mammograms are not always accurate. Even when done properly, mammograms fail to detect 10 to 15 percent of cancerous lumps, especially in the dense breasts of young women. And lumps can form in the time between mammograms. It's true that fast-growing tumors are rare, but they are also deadly. And they tend to be found more often in younger women, who may not be having yearly mammograms.

There are good reasons, too, not to rely solely on your gynecologist's breast examination. For one, he may not know what he's doing.

When a group of eighty doctors was tested for their ability to detect lumps in silicone models of female breasts, obstetrician-gynecologists performed more poorly than family doctors, surgeons, and internists. They detected only 40 percent of the hidden lumps. (The other doctors detected only 50 percent.) Even though they knew they were being observed, and they were told to treat the models as though they were real, the doctors spent a mean time of less than two minutes examining the breasts.

In real life, doctors spend even less time examining a patient's breasts for cancerous signs. One recent study found that the average length of time for a complete clinical breast examination was 1.8 minutes. This included examination of both breasts and counseling on breast self-examination.

Several studies show that spending more time on breast ex-
(continued)

amination pays off with the discovery of more lumps.

If you examine your own breasts, you can take all the time you want; you can become familiar with your breasts' anatomy; and you *can* learn to tell when there's a change in your breast that requires follow-up. Although there's no proof that women who do regular breast self-exam are less likely to die of breast cancer, there is evidence that women can be trained to find cancer at an early stage, which may translate into longer survival time, even cure.

———

lymph node involvement do not seem to predict whether there will be a recurrence of cancer in the breast.

Some women also receive chemotherapy, strong drugs that help to kill cancer cells circulating in the body. Not all doctors agree on who needs chemotherapy. They are particularly concerned that the treatment can cause serious side effects, including leukemia and heart disease. If your doctor recommends chemotherapy, find out why. Is it because the cancer has spread to your lymph nodes and so possibly to the rest of your body? Is it because your tumor was large, or because your cancer doesn't seem to be the type that responds to estrogen- or progestin-suppressing therapy, which can slow tumor growth? Ask your doctor what she hopes to accomplish with chemotherapy, and what she thinks will happen if you refuse the treatment.

Could Menstrual Cycle Affect Outcome of Breast Surgery?

If you're a premenopausal woman with newly discovered breast cancer, you may want to ask your doctor to schedule your surgery during the time of month that you're ovulating (midcycle) rather than shortly before or during your menstrual period.

Why? Because your hormone levels during ovulation may give you some natural immunity from cancer recurrence or spreading. At least, that's the finding of a small, and admittedly preliminary, study done by researchers in New York, California, and Minnesota (*The Lancet*, October 21, 1989).

The researchers looked at the medical records of forty-four premenopausal women who had had surgery for breast cancer and whose records indicated the date of their last menstrual period.

They found that women whose surgery was done midcycle (days 7–20) had significantly fewer, and later, recurrences of cancer, and survived longer than women whose surgery was done either a week before or during menstruation.

Eight of nineteen of the women who had surgery around the time of their periods had recurrences or spread of cancer, compared with three of twenty-two midcycle pa-tients. That's a four times greater risk. In all other risk factors, such as tumor size or lymph node involvement, the two groups were similar. (In scientific language, they were "controlled" for these factors.)

Researchers have noted a similar effect in female mice with laboratory-induced cancer. When the cancer was removed midcycle, it was less likely to have spread to the lungs a month later. Blood tests of the mice showed that the period of lowest cancer spread coincided with a time when important tumor-fighting white blood cells—natural killer cells—were at their peak of activity. These cells inhibit tumor cells from traveling through the body via the bloodstream and setting up housekeeping elsewhere.

"I suggest women show the journal article to their doctor," says William Hrushesky, M.D., the study's main researcher and a professor of medicine at Albany Medical College. "If it were my wife I'd advise her to wait a little while if necessary to have an excisional biopsy (in effect, a lumpectomy) during midcycle. After all, you are never more than two to three weeks away from a possibly safer period." While this study may turn out to be highly relevant, it is essential that you discuss and weigh all options with your practitioner.

163

Next Time, She Would Choose Mastectomy

"My doctor found a lump in my right breast during my annual physical. Although the mammogram showed nothing suspicious, a biopsy proved that the tumor was there and was malignant. I have since heard of several women who had the same experience. I wonder how many malignant tumors have been ignored on the strength of a negative mammogram.

"After the biopsy, my surgeon told me that we were looking at removal of half the breast with radiation therapy or removal of the whole breast without radiation therapy. The word *mastectomy* brought mental pictures of the way my mother was maimed by the old Halsted radical. When the oncologist who gave the second opinion said that I looked like a good candidate for a lumpectomy followed by radiation therapy and a five-year course of tamoxifen (an estrogen-suppressing drug), I felt very fortunate. I left his office with numerous publications on the subject of breast cancer. One of the booklets stated that some women *choose* mastectomy. I should have asked more questions then.

"One of the requirements of the route I had chosen was a lymph 'sampling' in the armpit. No one warned me how debilitating that 'sampling' would be. I lost twenty-six lymph nodes, and so much fluid built up in my lymph gland that I had to have it drained twice.

"After I had the lumpectomy and was committed to this course of action, only *then* did anyone discuss the hazards of radiation therapy. I was told that there would be some lung damage and some weakening of the rib cage. I felt I had no reasonable alternative but to go ahead, but I resented being put in this position.

"Once a week I saw the doctor. She told me I was progressing nicely. I *felt* terrible. After each of my daily radiation exposures my breast would become hot, heavy, and sore, eventually turning a dark, ugly red. I lived for the day I would take my last treatment.

"I am now taking tamoxifen twice a day and will be taking it for five years. It is expensive, as was the radiation therapy.

"If I had it to do over again I would seriously consider mastectomy. The lymph sample would then have been from the chest wall and, since my lymph nodes showed no cancer, I would not have needed radiation therapy. I am sixty-three years old and, for me, a breast is not a high priority item."

E.D.D.

Corpus Christi, Texas

CHAPTER FIVE

The Empowered Woman:

Staying in Charge of Your Care

Getting a Second Opinion

Getting a second opinion from a doctor who's totally independent of your first doctor may be the best way to avoid unnecessary tests, procedures, or surgery. Sure it's time, trouble, and money. But isn't it worth it if you end up avoiding an invasive and possibly risky medical procedure? Many medical insurance companies think it's well worth the effort. Some require a second opinion prior to surgery: if you don't get one, the insurance company may refuse to pay for your operation!

How often is unnecessary surgery recommended? Some of the best statistics come from researchers at Cornell Medical Center. Their studies, involving thousands of cases over a period of eight years, consistently showed that 25 percent of patients who were told they needed surgery were subsequently told by a second doctor that they didn't need it. A majority of these patients chose to believe the second doctor, didn't have the surgery, and survived very nicely without it.

Those same studies have found a drop in the percentage of recommended hysterectomies not confirmed by a second opinion, from 31 percent during the years 1972–1980 to 10 percent in 1981–1985, and to 9 percent in 1986–1988. The researchers note that as soon as a second opinion becomes mandatory prior to surgery (for insurance reimbursement), hysterectomy rates drop.

Some women's health groups contend that the recommendation rate for unnecessary hysterectomies is higher. Some say it's still about 33 percent, and at least one group (HERS) thinks it's closer to 90 percent. They cite the fact that only 10 percent of hysterectomies are performed for life-threatening conditions such as cancer or uncontrollable bleeding. Some 90 percent of hysterectomies are considered "elective." In other words, they are non-lifesaving operations that may or may not improve a woman's quality of life.

When should you get a second opinion? Definitely get one anytime you're told to have surgery. But don't limit the search for a second opinion to procedures that involve surgery. Many types of tests and procedures are risky, even though they are not invasive. Ask another doctor for assurance about the need for any procedure or treatment regimen that concerns you, even if you have discussed it at length with your first doctor.

Where should you get a second opinion? You should know that a lot of second-opinion doctors recommended by first-opinion doctors turn out to be professional ditto marks. They're not all that helpful in terms of thinking differently about your problem or exploring other options. This may be because they don't want to offend their friend, your first doctor, by disagreeing with his opinion. Or it may be because the second-opinion doctor may not take time to gather much new or additional information of his own. He'll discuss your case with your first doctor, read the medical records your first doctor has written, and look at the results of tests your first doctor has already done. The information the second-opinion doctor gets may already be biased in a certain direction, and his diagnosis will be based on that information.

So find yourself a doctor for a fair and original opinion by asking around or calling a local hospital for referrals. (You may want to call the chief of the department of obstetrics and gynecology at the nearest large hospital.) Check the *Directory of Medical Specialists* in your local library's reference section. Or call the government's toll-free Second Surgical Opinion Hotline. The number is 1-800-638-6833 (in Maryland, 1-800-492-6603). They'll give you a phone number in your area to call for a local referral to a second-opinion doctor specializing in your health problem. Do select carefully. This is not the time to let your fingers do the walking!

You can simply ask your first doctor for a copy of your medical records and take them along with you to the second-opinion doctor, or have them mailed prior to your visit.

You may want to see a second-opinion doctor without telling him that's why you're there. If so, you'll tell him nothing about the findings of your first doctor and let him do his own medical history and tests. One problem with this is that certain tests may be repeated unnecessarily. And sometimes tests repeated too soon after the initial tests can be inaccurate. This is certainly the case for a second Pap smear done too soon after the first, and it's also true for some kinds of biopsies, because if a lesion is small, some or most of the abnormal cells are removed during the first smear or biopsy, and they take time to grow back. (Sometimes they never grow back.)

The ideal second-opinion situation, then, may be a competent doctor, found by you, who reviews your first doctor's records and test results, and repeats or adds what tests you and she deem necessary. The second-opinion doctor might confirm the original diagnosis. Or she might contradict the first doctor's conclusions and thus create some doubt about the need for surgery. You might require a third, tie-breaking opinion.

Below are some gynecological or breast cancer procedures for which you often need a second, and even a third, opinion. Why? Because these procedures are controversial. They may once have been standard practice but are now considered obsolete and unnecessary except in special cases. Or doctors may have widely differing opinions as to whether they are necessary or effective.

- *Hysterectomy for any reason, and especially when recommended for the following conditions, for which it is not appropriate*:
- for many cases of fibroid tumors
- as a means of permanent sterilization (hysterectomy has a complication rate ten to twenty times higher than tubal ligation)

167

- to prevent cancer
- for cervicitis (inflammation of the cervix)
- for mildly abnormal patterns of uterine bleeding
- for most cases of menstrual pain or premenstrual syndrome
- for abortion (during the first and second trimesters)

New diagnostic and surgical techniques such as hysteroscopy, laparoscopy, and ultrasound make it possible to avoid or delay hysterectomies that would have been routine not so long ago.

- *Ovary removal for any reason except ovarian cancer*
  Your ovaries don't necessarily need to be removed if you are having a hysterectomy, even if the hysterectomy is for uterine cancer. Some surgeons take a cavalier attitude toward ovaries, thinking that hormone replacement therapy will make up for loss of hormone-producing organs. It does somewhat, but it's not the real thing. Tell your doctor ahead of time that you want to preserve your ovaries if at all possible, even if it's emergency surgery. Write it on your surgical consent form. If you are having surgery for a possible ovarian cyst, tell the doctor you want only the cyst removed, and again, note this on your surgical consent form.

- *Dilation and curettage (D&C) for most conditions*
  D&C used to be the third most common operation in the United States. This technique of dilating the cervix, then scraping the uterine lining with a spoon-shaped instrument, a curette, was used both to diagnose and to treat problems involving suspicious or irregular bleeding.
  For diagnosis, D&C has been replaced by two better procedures: hysteroscopy, which allows the doctor to view the inside of the uterus; and aspiration endometrial biopsy, a quick procedure in which a plastic tube is inserted into the uterus to suck out a bit of tissue for microscopic examination. And D&C is no longer considered standard care for irregular bleeding.
  D&Cs are still used if the cervix is too scarred to be dilated for aspiration biopsy; if an aspiration biopsy shows suspicious or uncertain results; and sometimes to remove incompletely passed products of conception, such as after a miscarriage or birth. But in most cases it's wise to explore what may be better,

safer options that run less risk of uterine perforation and infection.

- *Cautery (heat) or cryosurgery (freezing) for cervical erosion*

  There is no evidence that cervical erosion leads to cervical cancer, although some doctors say it does and will want to treat it.

  Any cervical abnormality should first be biopsied and cultured to see if it is being caused by a virus (such as human papilloma virus) or other infection. If it is, most doctors will treat it with cautery or cryosurgery. If it is found to be benign, nonspecific cervical erosion, which sometimes occurs after childbirth or other times during a woman's life and often disappears spontaneously, it need not be treated.

- *Partially cutting nerves to the uterus and pelvis for pain (known as presacral neurectomy)*

  This fifty-year-old operation is back in vogue again in some parts of the country (especially Texas and other parts of the South) for relieving the pain of endometriosis or severe menstrual cramps. It's frequently done during laparoscopic laser surgery. The doctors who perform it say it has a 70 percent chance of relieving some symptoms. But other doctors remain unconvinced of the effectiveness of this procedure.

- *Prophylactic surgery of any kind*

  Prophylactic, or preventive, surgery is done to try to avoid the occurrence of cancer (not its recurrence). Very rare, it is most often recommended to people who have a strong family history of cancer, which means that two or more close relatives (especially the mother) had the same kind of cancer at an earlier-than-usual age.

  Among women, ovary and breast removal are the two most common kinds of prophylactic surgery. The problems with this type of surgery are that in some cases it's done on women whose odds against getting cancer are still pretty good, and even when the ovaries or breast are removed, cancer can develop in adjacent tissues. Careful monitoring may be a better option.

  "The only time I've done a prophylactic oophorectomy [removal of ovaries] is when I'm doing a hysterectomy on a woman who's close to menopause who has a strong family history of ovarian cancer," says Dr. Utian.

- *Surgery for symptomless fibroid tumors of the uterus*

   Not all fibroid tumors have to be removed. Many do not, and some can be treated with drugs that shrink the tumors. You need to discuss all your options, and your needs, with a doctor knowledgeable in this area. There are many factors to consider in your decision, as Lynn Payer points out in her book *How to Avoid a Hysterectomy*. Most doctors like to remove fibroids when the uterus has reached the size of a grapefruit (about a three-month pregnancy size). Doctors say this is because surgery becomes more difficult, and symptoms are more likely to develop, if the fibroids get much bigger than that.

   If you're having nonsymptomatic fibroids removed because they may be hampering your ability to become pregnant, consider having the surgery done by an infertility expert. This doctor is skilled in techniques that minimize surgical scarring. (Surgical scars can also interfere with your ability to become pregnant.)

- *Radiation therapy for any kind of pelvic cancer*

   Radiation therapy may be necessary prior to surgery to shrink large tumors, or after surgery, instead of chemotherapy, to kill lingering cancer cells. But, when possible, most doctors prefer surgery over radiation treatment for any kind of pelvic cancer. This is because surgery is less likely than radiation to damage the bowels, ovaries, bladder, or other pelvic organs.

   Make sure you clearly understand your options. Your best bet: discuss your treatment beforehand with a gynecological or medical oncologist, a doctor who can plan and coordinate your cancer surgery plus any radiation treatment or chemotherapy you may need.

- *A mastectomy rather than lumpectomy for breast cancer*

   A mastectomy removes the entire breast. A lumpectomy removes only the cancerous tumor plus a bit of surrounding tissue. Although studies show that women with early breast cancer who have lumpectomies live just as long as women who have mastectomies, some doctors continue to recommend mastectomies to women who are candidates for lumpectomy.

Your best bet: see a medical oncologist before you agree to any treatment for breast cancer. These days, most breast cancer is viewed as a systemic (whole body) disease. Its treatment extends beyond surgery, to radiation, hormone treatment, or chemotherapy. A medical oncologist will begin planning your treatment program even before surgery, working with both your surgeon and a radiotherapist.

- *A Halsted radical mastectomy for breast cancer*

    This mutilating breast surgery removes not only the breast, but a good portion of the muscles of the chest wall. It hasn't been recommended for years, except in rare cases where cancer has spread into the chest. Some other forms of radical mastectomy are still done.

- *Surgical removal of a breast cyst that has returned after needle aspiration of fluid*

    Doctors treat painful breast cysts by drawing out fluid with a needle, which collapses the cyst. But if the cyst refills with fluid, some doctors like to remove it, just as they would a solid lump. This is unnecessary; cysts are unlikely to be harboring a malignancy. A cyst can be aspirated as many times as a patient wants. Of course, sometimes it's the patient who insists a cyst be removed. No lump should be assumed to be a cyst without a confirming ultrasound or a mammogram.

Safe and Unsafe Drugs for Women

In the past, women and their unborn children were virtual guinea pigs when it came to prescription drugs, including hormones. Long-term side effects, especially on the developing fetus, weren't carefully studied. And nobody suspected that the harmful effects of a drug given during pregnancy, such as DES, would show up years later in a woman's grown children.

Today, it's less likely, but still possible, to be the victim of a drug that should never have been marketed in the first place. Your bigger concern, though, is being given drugs that are not necessary or not appropriate for you, or taking several drugs at one time and suffering multiple side effects. It's common for a doctor to mistake the side effects of a drug for a new ailment, and to prescribe an additional drug rather than stopping the first drug, Sidney Wolfe, M.D., points out in his book *Worst Pills, Best Pills* (Public Citizen Health Research Group, Washington, D.C., 1988). The result can be a confusion of symptoms, including mental problems, that land people in hospitals or nursing homes, or even kill them.

Still, drugs can be very helpful, even lifesaving, and because all but the most diehard of us will take them occasionally, the question is: What do we need to know to stay out of trouble?

First, ask your doctor:

■ *Is it absolutely necessary that I take this drug? Is there a chance that I'll die if I don't take it, or have symptoms so uncomfortable that I'll wish I were dead? Or is taking this drug a choice on my part, something that may improve the quality of my life? In other words, why am I being given this drug? Exactly what symptom is it for, and what is it supposed to do in my body?*

■ *How long has this drug been on the market?*

Most new drugs are required by the U.S. Food and Drug Administration to be tested before they are given approval to be sold, but newer drugs (on the market for three years or less) are sometimes discovered to have unforeseen side effects. Since older drugs have survived a shakedown period, their side effects are generally known. But an older drug may not work as well as a newer drug. And it may have more side effects. So you'll need to ask:

■ *Is there another drug that can do the same thing but is safer?*

■ *Could any nondrug treatments work just as well?*

A crucial question to ask is:

■ *What are the side effects of this drug?*

Unfortunately, almost every drug has some side effects, some severe, some minor, some common, some rare. A drug may have so many possible side effects that your doctor can't recite them all—only the most common or serious ones. If you have time, it's a good idea to read about a drug before you fill the prescription. You can look the drug up in the *Physician's Desk Reference* (44th edition, Medical Economics Company, Oradell, N.J., 1990), available at most public libraries. Besides indications for use, and side effects, this book includes the FDA's use-in-pregnancy rating and potential-for-abuse (addiction) rating. You can obtain the same data by getting an information sheet on the drug from your pharmacist. You may want to read it before you have the prescription filled, in case you change your mind about taking the drug. Ask the pharmacist about anything on the sheet you don't understand, or call your doctor. Take the sheet home with you to refer to later, if necessary.

As with a test or surgery, you should be thinking:

■ *Do the benefits of taking this drug outweigh the possible risks?*

■ *Are there safer alternatives?*

You may decide to try a drug, see if you develop side effects, and decide if they're tolerable. Some side effects, however, such as kidney or liver damage, may have no symptoms until the organs are seriously harmed. If you develop side effects troubling enough to consider stopping the drug, call your doctor. She may agree that you should stop it, cut you to a lower dose, or switch you to a different drug.

Always ask:

■ *How should this drug be taken?*

Ask for written instructions if necessary. Then take the drug according to the directions. You may need to drink plenty of fluids to avoid kidney damage, or to take it with meals to avoid stomach irritation. If you're supposed to stay out of the sun—do so! Otherwise you could end up with a life-threatening sunburn. If you're using a vaginal cream or suppository, ask if you should avoid sexual intercourse, use a different form of birth control, or use sanitary napkins rather than tampons.

If you stop taking a drug, or don't take it the way you were directed, and your problem continues or returns, confess. Tell your doctor you did not take the drug according to directions. It could save you a lot of time and money, and tests or treatments you may not need.

Always ask yourself if you could be pregnant. If there's even a remote chance, ask your doctor:

■ *Is this drug known to cause birth defects?*

Drugs that cause birth defects often do so very early in pregnancy. If you think you're pregnant, it's best to stop taking any drug, including over-the-counter items and fertility-inducing drugs, until you check with your doctor.

Some drugs can cause breast enlargement or tenderness, vaginal or rectal itching, vaginal dryness, decreased sexual desire or decreased sexual ability, heat stress, fatigue, and dizziness. Many drugs can cause depression, and a fair number also cause confusion, irritability, and mood swings. Before you're treated for any physical problem, you'll want to discuss possible side effects of the drugs you are already taking with your doctor. These should include prescription and over-the-counter drugs, illegal drugs, alcohol, herbal remedies, and vitamin-mineral supplements. If your doctor disagrees with your suspicion that a drug is causing your symptoms, you may want to try stopping the drug for a time to see if your symptoms improve. It's best to do this with your doctor's supervision, though. Some drugs need to be decreased gradually, and in some cases, the symptoms for which the drug is being taken can flare up.

What are the top ten drugs prescribed for women? The top ten drugs gynecologists prescribe? The data research companies that crunch numbers for the drug industry have these figures, but they won't release them to just anyone. They are "proprietary information," available only to drug manufacturers who are willing to pay to find out which medical specialists

174

are prescribing which kinds of drugs, and to whom. These figures help drug companies plan their marketing strategies so they can sell more drugs.

It seems safe enough to assume that gynecologists prescribe more oral contraceptives and menopausal replacement hormones than do other doctors, but as for painkillers, antibiotics, or tranquilizers, there's no way to know for sure.

Below are drugs commonly prescribed to women (or recommended, if they are over-the-counter drugs) and some of their possible side effects.

Oral Contraceptives (Birth Control Pills)

Oral contraceptives—containing estrogen and progestins—are the most effective form of birth control available. They are 98 percent effective (this means two out of every one hundred women using them will become pregnant, usually because they missed some pills). Unfortunately, this effectiveness comes at the cost of a wide range of side effects. The most serious include blood-clotting problems, heart attack and stroke, gallbladder disease, and noncancerous liver tumors. Most studies attempting to link oral contraceptives and cancer have been negative. There may be a weak link with cervical cancer, and possibly a slightly increased risk of breast cancer.

Common, less serious side effects include acne or unsightly hair growth, weight gain, depression, breast tenderness or enlargement, premenstrual-like symptoms (fluid retention, nervousness, irritability, headache), decreased sexual desire, fatigue, nausea, vomiting, and bloating. Oral contraceptives can also cause deficiencies of the nutrients riboflavin, folate, and vitamins B-6, B-12, and C.

If you smoke, and especially if you're age thirty-five or older, you should not use oral contraceptives. If you do, your chances of having a stroke or heart attack are significantly increased.

Oral contraceptives come in a wide range of dosages, both for estrogen and progestins. The "mini-Pill" contains only progestins. Its advantage is fewer estrogen-related side effects. Its disadvantage is a greater chance of contraceptive failure, especially if you miss a dose or two.

In most cases, your doctor will start you on a low-dose pill and then adjust your prescription according to any side effects you report.

According to Harold Silverman, Pharm. D., author of *The Women's Drugstore* (Dell Publishing, New York, 1985):

- Too much estrogen can cause nausea, bloating, cervical polyps, irritability, vaginal itching and mucous discharge, headaches, high blood pressure, tiredness, reduced sexual desire, breast fullness or tenderness, and weight gain, among other symptoms.

- Too little estrogen in relationship to progestin can cause vaginal bleeding during early or midcycle, spotting, or unusually light menstrual bleeding.

- Too much progestin can cause increased appetite, weight gain, tiredness, unusually light menstrual bleeding, oily scalp and acne, depression, loss of hair, reduction in breast size, or frequent vaginal infections.

- Too little progestin in relationship to estrogen can cause breakthrough bleeding late in the cycle or a missed period.

Other Forms of Birth Control

Are you getting some other form of contraception, or using an over-the-counter item? Ask your doctor about its effectiveness. He should be able to tell you how many women out of one hundred become pregnant in one year while using that form of contraception. Have him compare its effectiveness with other forms of birth control, to give you an idea of how likely you are to become pregnant while using that particular contraceptive. Some forms of birth control, such as the contraceptive sponge, work better as a woman becomes familiar with it. Ask your doctor if that's the case with the method of birth control you are selecting. If so, you may want to use a backup contraceptive for the first few months. Don't leave the doctor's office without being absolutely sure how to use any method of birth control. If you're getting a diaphragm, you should put it in yourself, have the doctor check its placement, and take it out yourself, until you're confident that you're doing it right.

176

Menopausal Replacement Hormones (Estrogen, Progestins, and Androgens)

Because the decision whether to take menopausal replacement hormones is complex and depends on individual risk factors, we suggest you see "Hormone Replacement Therapy," page 121, for a more detailed discussion.

There's disagreement on the possible side effects of replacement hormones, especially when it comes to cancer and heart disease. As detailed in Chapter 4, an older woman's risk for endometrial cancer is actually lower than normal if she takes both estrogen and progestins in the correct dosage. This is because she continues to menstruate and thus sheds the endometrium each month. Her risk for breast cancer may be slightly increased if she takes a high-dosage pill, although many doctors dispute that finding. As for blood clots, heart disease, and stroke, studies are mixed, with some finding no risk, some finding a slightly increased risk, and some finding less risk. Certainly more research needs to be done in this area.

In addition to these risks, other possible side effects include menstrual irregularities, swollen and tender breasts, fluid retention and high blood pressure, nausea, colitis, dizziness, depression, changes in sexual desire, hair loss or hair growth, itching, skin rashes, and patchy discolorations of the skin.

Androgens are male hormones given much less frequently than estrogen or progestins. They can cause masculinization (hair growth, enlargement of the clitoris, and deepening of voice, among other symptoms). These side effects can be controlled through proper dosage, and by giving the drug by injection rather than orally.

Antibiotics (Tetracycline, Erythromycin, Penicillin, Ampicillin, and Many Others)

These infection-fighting drugs have wide usage: in gynecology, they're prescribed for pelvic inflammatory disease and other sexually transmitted diseases, urinary tract infections, and some vaginal infections. Antifungal drugs (miconazole, trade name: Monistat; clotrimazde, trade name: Gyne-Lotrim) and antiviral drugs (acyclovir, trade name: Zovirax) may also be used.

Unfortunately, antibiotics are also overwhelmingly mis-prescribed, according to congressional hearings and numerous academic studies. As *Worst Pills, Best Pills* points out, the majority of antibiotics are given in situations in which the infection cannot be treated by any antibiotic or a more effective and appropriate antibiotic should be used instead. Mispres-cribing of antibiotics can pose real threats, especially to older adults. Side effects include stomach irritation, diarrhea, liver and kidney problems, and growth in the body of antibiotic-resistant strains of bacteria, which can then be passed on to others. Most doctors agree that antibiotics, sometimes in com-binations and in large doses, are necessary to wipe out pelvic inflammatory disease.

Many women develop vaginal yeast infections while taking antibiotics; the drug wipes out the normal bacteria in the vagina, allowing yeast to flourish. It can also cause diarrhea because it kills beneficial bacteria in the intestines. And it can cause yeast infections in the mouth and throat. Eating live-culture yogurt, taking acidophilus tablets, and using a yeast-killing vaginal cream during and for a few weeks after anti-biotic use will help keep these symptoms under control.

─────── **Vaginitis Drugs (Miconazole, Clotrimazole, Diclotrimazole, Terconazole, Nystatin)**

Creams and suppositories containing miconazole (Monis-tat-7 and other brand names) and related compounds are con-sidered equally effective for treating occasional vaginal yeast infections. Used correctly, any brand a doctor prescribes will knock out an overgrowth of yeast in about 90 percent of women, with virtually no side effects. One out of every ten women, however, will soon have a recurrence, and many of those with recurrences will develop chronic yeast overgrowth, which may be treated with drugs and dietary changes.

Vaginal infections caused by bacteria (called bacterial va-ginosis) are usually treated with metronidazole (brand name:

Flagyl.) This drug has a number of possible side effects, including nausea, headache, loss of appetite, bad metallic taste in the mouth, and depression. It has been shown to cause cancer in laboratory animals given massive doses, but most doctors believe its cancer-causing potential is very low in women given therapeutic doses. (It is never prescribed during pregnancy.) Oral antibiotics may also be used for some kinds of bacterial vaginosis.

Recurrent vaginal infections need special attention. The organism or organisms causing the infection should be identified by a culture (growing them in the laboratory from a vaginal smear). Some organisms are antibiotic-resistant, and their treatment requires very specific antibiotics or a combination of antibiotics. Since many bacterial infections are sexually transmitted, a woman's sex partners may also need to be treated, whether or not they have symptoms.

Pain-Relieving Drugs (Aspirin, Acetominophen, Ibuprofen, and Others)

For menstrual cramps, drugs that have an antiprostaglandin effect work best. These drugs counteract prostaglandin, a pain- and inflammation-causing chemical produced in the body (and by the uterus) that causes muscle cramping. Both ibuprofen and aspirin are antiprostaglandins. Acetaminophen (Tylenol) is not.

According to *Consumer Reports* (February 1987), studies show that ibuprofen provides complete or significant relief for 75 percent of women with menstrual pain. Aspirin may work just as well for many women, at much less cost. Ibuprofen is somewhat easier on the stomach than aspirin. Avoid ibuprofen products marketed for menstrual pain, *Consumer Reports* recommends. They cost much more than other, identical ibuprofen products.

If over-the-counter drugs do not relieve your menstrual pain, your doctor may prescribe stronger antiprostaglandins. Be aware that all these drugs increase your risk of gastrointestinal bleeding.

──────── *Estrogen-Inhibiting Drugs (Tamoxifen, Danazol)*

Tamoxifen (Nolvadex) is used after surgery to treat women with cancer, especially breast cancer, that grows in response to estrogen (it is estrogen receptor positive). Tamoxifen competes with estrogen in the body, effectively "locking it out" of cancer and other cells. It's preferred over other hormones that do the same thing because it has fewer side effects and is just as effective. It causes hot flashes, and one in four women have nausea and vomiting while taking this drug.

Danazol (Danocrine) is a synthetic male hormone that decreases the production of estrogen by the ovaries. It's sometimes used instead of oral contraceptives for the treatment of endometriosis. While it's effective at shrinking patches of endometrial tissue, it's usually not prescribed for more than nine months at a time, because of many possible side effects. They include acne, swelling of legs and arms, increased body hair, decreased breast size, weight gain, flushing, sweating, nervousness, and liver damage.

──────── *Ovulation-Inducing Drugs (Clomiphene Citrate, Menotrophins, Human Chorionic Gonadotrophin, Bromocriptine)*

Clomiphene citrate (Clomid) is usually the first drug a doctor will use to try to coax a woman's ovary to release an egg. In 70 percent of women, this drug does work. Most women who will respond to clomiphene citrate by ovulating do so within the first month or so of treatment. For women who don't initially respond, however, some doctors will continue the drug in increasing dosages for up to six months. Clomiphene citrate is not usually responsible for multiple births. The actual incidence of multiple births among women taking this drug is 5 to 10 percent, and most of those births are twins. (Higher than normal dosages is usually the cause.) Side effects are infrequent and usually minor. They include hot flashes, enlargement of the ovaries, abdominal bloating or pain, breast tenderness, and other symptoms.

If clomiphene citrate fails to produce ovulation, your doctor may try stronger drugs, such as menotrophins (Pergonal) or human chorionic gonadotrophins. It's important that these powerful drugs be given only by a doctor experienced in their use, in most cases a reproduction endocrinologist, because they can cause rapid development of fluid buildup in the lungs, ovary enlargement, and multiple births if they are misused. Both drugs are given by injection.

Bromocriptine (Parlodel) is used only when a woman fails to ovulate because of too-high levels of prolactin, a hormone that ordinarily stimulates the production of breast milk. High prolactin levels are usually caused by a problem with the pituitary gland in the brain. More than 95 percent of women will respond to bromocriptine treatment with lower prolactin levels, and 80 to 90 percent will ovulate. Side effects are extremely common but are usually mild if the dosage of the drug is increased gradually. They include nasal stuffiness, nausea, headache, dizziness, fatigue, abdominal cramps, and other symptoms. Serious but rare reactions include dramatic changes in blood pressure, seizures, strokes, heart attacks, blood clots, and psychosis.

Tranquilizers (Benzodiazepines)

Although they are called "minor" tranquilizers (as opposed to major tranquilizers used primarily in the treatment of psychosis), mood-altering drugs such as Xanax, Ativan, Valium, and Librium all have the potential for addiction and abuse. According to *The New Our Bodies, Ourselves*, physicians prescribe more than two-thirds of all legal psychoactive drugs to women, and more than one million women report dependence on them.

Tranquilizers are not meant to be used to "treat" the ordinary stress of daily life. They may be appropriately used for short-term crisis situations, truly disabling depression or anxiety, and some physical ailments. Research shows that use of these drugs for more than four months increases the potential for addiction. It's important to withdraw gradually from a tranquilizer, with your doctor's guidance. Stopping abruptly can

181

lead to withdrawal symptoms such as convulsions, tremor, abdominal and muscle cramps, vomiting, and sweating.

Besides addiction, these drugs can also cause drowsiness, fatigue, confusion, constipation, depression, headache, skin rash, slurred speech, and tremor. Paradoxical reactions, including overexcitability, hallucinations, insomnia, and rage, have also been reported.

——— *Tips to Save and Survive*

- State the reason or reasons for your office visit at the time that you make your appointment. This way, the doctor's office manager will schedule your appointment for an appropriate amount of time. Don't expect a lot of extra time if you tack additional health problems onto the end of an office visit with a "Hey, doc, while we're at it . . ." If these health problems are of enough concern to you to want to discuss them with your doctor, mention them when you make your appointment.

- If you're concerned that you won't speak as clearly or logically as you'd like to during a doctor's visit, try writing down your thoughts and symptoms ahead of time in an orderly fashion, revising them a few times if necessary. Make a copy of the finished version for the doctor to review as you talk together.

- If you call your doctor's office with questions and the receptionist seems rude or abrupt, consider that it may not be a good time to call. Ask "Can you talk now, or are you busy?" If she says she's busy, ask "Will you call me back when you're not busy?" or "When would be a good time for me to call back?"

- If you expect to be seen on time, show up on time. Call if you are going to be late. And if your doctor is habitually late for appointments, call before you leave to find out what time you can expect to be seen.

- Refuse any kind of surgical procedure to correct sexual dysfunctioning unless it is recommended by a very reputable sex therapist and verified by at least two independent medical opinions. In most cases, sexual dysfunction is not caused by anatomical problems in the genital area, and surgery to "correct" or "optimize" sexual responsiveness can backfire badly.

• If you're having a test, procedure, or surgery done in a teaching hospital, make sure you know who exactly is going to be doing it. If your regular doctor plans to allow a doctor-in-training (a resident) to do the procedure, or parts of it, under supervision, it should be done only with your permission.

• Don't expect medical care to substitute for healthy living. If you're smoking, eating poorly, overweight, sedentary, under stress and not getting enough sleep, don't expect your doctor to fix you in one visit. You may need the help of a nutritionist, psychologist, or weight-loss or smoking-cessation program.

• If you have menstrual cramps that are more severe than normal within a few months after an abortion, cone biopsy, or any other cervical or uterine procedure, you may have developed cervical stenosis (scarring that leads to narrowing of the cervical opening). Your gynecologist may be able to dilate the cervical opening in a simple in-office procedure.

• If you're having trouble understanding your doctor's description of a procedure or condition, ask if she has a model of that body part, or a photograph or drawing. (She may even be able to draw it for you.) Ask to see the instruments your doctor will use.

• Ask to see your mammogram or any other kind of X ray or medical image that's taken of you. It may help you to understand the doctor's explanation of your condition.

• Once you find a good mammography center, stick with it. Have your mammogram done at the same place, and ask to have it read by the same radiologist each year. This way, subtle changes in breast tissue are less likely to be overlooked.

• If you think you're pregnant, get an early pregnancy test. If you're considering an abortion, the sooner you have it done, the less risky the procedure. Abortions are relatively safe. The complication rate is 1 percent for an abortion done during the first three months of pregnancy (a first trimester abortion). But the risks increase after that time. Most doctors will do vacuum aspiration abortions at up to twelve weeks, and dilation and evacuation (D&E) under general anesthesia at thirteen to eighteen weeks. If you're having trouble making a timely decision, call Planned Parenthood, a women's health clinic, or your local hospital, which may have on staff a pregnancy counselor or social worker.

- If you're using oral contraceptives, have your blood pressure checked every six months. Studies show that women who use the Pill are three times more likely to develop high blood pressure than non-Pill users. High blood pressure is associated with heart attacks and strokes. Lower-dose pills produce fewer of these side effects.

- If you use a diaphragm and have recurrent urinary tract infections, have the size of your diaphragm checked. You may need a smaller size.

- Take an iron supplement if you are using an intrauterine device (IUD) as your form of birth control. Women with IUDs lose twice the amount of blood during menstruation as those using other forms of birth control.

- Get a blood test for diabetes if you have recurrent vaginal yeast infections. Diabetes or a prediabetic condition can change the chemistry of the vagina, allowing yeast to proliferate. Diabetes is best treated early on, with changes in diet, weight loss, exercise, or drugs, if necessary.

- Don't neglect your health because you're broke. Planned Parenthood or a neighborhood or hospital clinic may offer pay-what-you-can gynecologic health care. Save money by asking your doctor to write you a generic prescription. If you're really broke and know you can't afford to have a prescription filled, tell your doctor. He may have free samples of the drug or medication on hand.

A Guide to Medical Abbreviations

Medical people seem to love to abbreviate, especially on your chart and medical records. It's faster and easier for them, but barely decipherable to the unaccustomed eye. This means that when you look at your chart and records (something you ought to do regularly), you are shut off from what your doctor is thinking about you and your condition. Abbreviations are one more obstacle blocking your participation in your own care.

Note the following medical abbreviations. Many are frequently associated with gynecologic procedures. If you come across others in your readings or discussions, ask a nurse or doctor to translate. Don't be bowled over or too impressed by technical jive talk. Your body and your life may be at stake. Even the most revered medical figure who can't (or worse yet, won't) speak in an understandable fashion is wrong. Tell your doctor you want to be spoken to in everyday, direct, and totally honest English. Communicating is the most important first step in a healing relationship.

a = before
aa. = of each
a.c. = before meals
Ad. = to, up to
ADL = activities of daily living
ad lib = as needed, as desired
AMA = against medical advice
Ap. = appendicitis
Aq. = water
B.E. = barium enema
b.i.d. = twice a day
Dl. time – bleeding time
B.M. = bowel movement
B.P. = blood pressure
BRP = bathroom privileges
Bx = biopsy
c̄ = with
CA = cancer; cardiac arrest
c.b.c. = complete blood cell count
C.C. = chief complaint; current complaint
Chol = cholesterol
CIN = cervical intraepithelial neoplasm
Cl. time = clotting time

CNS = central nervous system
Comp. = compound; compress
cont rem = continue the medicine
CT = computerized tomography; chlamydia trachomatis, clotting time
Cx. = cervix; convex
CXR = chest X ray
d = day
d.d. = give
D&C = dilation and curettage
dd in d = from day to day
D&E = dilation and evacuation (second trimester abortion)
DES = diethylstilbestrol
dexter = the right
disp. = dispense
Div. = divide
DM = diabetes mellitus; diabetic mother
D.O. = Doctor of Osteopathy
dos = dose

Dur. dolor. = while pain lasts

Dx = diagnosis

ECC = endocervical curettage

ECG or EKG = electrocardiogram

emp = as directed

ER = estrogen receptor (assay); emergency room

ERT = estrogen replacement therapy

F.A.C.O.G. = Fellow of the American College of Obstetrics and Gynecology

F.A.C.S. = Fellow of the American College of Surgeons

febris = fever

FH = family history

GA = general anesthesia; general appearance; gestational age

GB = gallbladder

GC = gonorrhea

GI = gastrointestinal

GIFT = gamete intrafallopian transfer (part of the in vitro fertilization process)

GnRH = gonadotrophin releasing hormone

gravida = a pregnant woman

gravidism = pregnancy, or the sum of symptoms, signs, and conditions associated with it

GU = genitourinary; gastric ulcer

GYN = gynecology

h = hour

Hb or Hgb = hemoglobin

HCT = hematocrit

HMO = health maintenance organization

HPI = history of present illness

HPV = human papilloma virus

HRT = hormone replacement therapy; heart rate

h.s. = at bedtime, before retiring

Hx = history

ICU = intensive care unit

I&D = incision and drainage

I.M. = intramuscular; infectious mononucleosis; internal medicine

I&O = intake and output (measure fluids going into and out of the body)

in d. = daily

IUD = intrauterine device

I.V. = intravenous; intrauterine death

IVF = in vitro fertilization

L. = left

liq = liquid

L.M.P. = last menstrual period

m et n = morning and night

mg. = milligram

M.D. = medical doctor

MI = heart attack (myocardial infarction); menstrual induction

Mor. dict. = in the manner directed

neg. = negative

no. = number

non rep; nr = do not repeat

NP = nurse practitioner; new patient; no pain

NPO = non per os (nothing by mouth)

NS = normal saline; nervous system; no specimen

NSR = normal heart rate; not seen regularly

N&V = nausea and vomiting

O_2 = oxygen

o = none

OB. = obstetrics; occult bleeding

OC = oral contraceptive

O.D. = once a day

OOB = out of bed

OPD = outpatient department

O.R. = operating room

p = after

P = pain; postpartum; progesterone

Para = number of births

path. = pathology

p.c. = after meals

P.C. = patient care; post-coital, present complaint

PE = physical examination; pulmonary embolus

PI = present illness; patient's interest; perinatal injury; primary infection

PID = pelvic inflammatory disease

Pil. = pill

P.O. = per os (by mouth)

Post. = posterior

post-op = postoperative, after the operation

PR = progesterone receptor (assay); pulse rate; rectally; pregnancy

p.r.n. = as needed; as often as necessary

PMS = premenstrual syndrome; People's Medical Society

Prog. = prognosis

pt = patient

PT = physical therapy

PTA = prior to admission

Px = prognosis

q = every; each

q.h. = every hour (q4h = every four hours; q8h = every eight hours; and so on)

q.i.d. = four times a day

qn = every night

qod = every other day

q.s. = proper amount, quantity sufficient

qv = as much as desired

R = right; roentgen; rectal; regular; relapse

rbc = red blood cell

R.B.C. = red blood cell; red blood cell count

Rep. = repeat

R.N. = registered nurse

ROM = range of motion

RR = respiratory rate; recovery room

RT = radiation therapy; reaction time; right

Rx = prescription; therapy; treatment

s = without

S&A = sugar and acetone (a urine test for diabetes)

SC = subcutaneous

SH = social history

SICU = surgical intensive care unit

sing. = of each

SOP = standard operating procedure

ss. = one half

S&S = signs and symptoms

SSE = soapsuds enema; saline solution enema; skin self-exam

stat. = right away, immediately

STD = sexually transmitted disease

suppos = suppository

Sx = symptoms

tere = rub

t.i.d. = three times a day

TPR = temperature, pulse, and respiration

TSS = toxic shock syndrome

Tx = treatment; traction

UTI = urinary tract infection

V.D. = venereal disease (sexually transmitted disease)

VS = vital signs; voluntary sterilization

W.B.C. = white blood cells; white blood cell count

ZIFT = zygote intrafallopian transfer (part of the in vitro fertilization process)

↑ = increase

↗ = increasing

↓ = decrease

↙ = decreasing

→ = leads to

← = resulting from

♂ = male

♀ = female

———— The Key to Translating Medical Terms

You need a tool to take all the pieces—the prefixes, roots, and suffixes that comprise so many medical terms—and weld them into understandable words and sentences. The following lists will help you to do this. They include the bits and pieces, roots and modifiers, most commonly used by the medical profession to produce terminology guaranteed to mystify.

First are the prefixes—the short bits that are attached to the front of words to indicate the wheres, ifs, and how muches:

a, an = not, without

ab = away from

ante = before

anti = against

colpo = vagina

contra = against, counter to

cry = cold

dia = through or passing through, going apart, between, across

dys = painful, difficult

e = out from

ecto = outside of, outer, exterior

endo = within

epi = upon, on, over

erythr = red

eso = inside

exo = outside of

hyper = above, increased, excessive

hypo = under, below, deficient

in = not (*n* changes to *l, m,* or *r* when it precedes roots that be-

gin with these let-
ters)
infra = below
inter = between
intra = within
leuco, leuko = white
macro = large
mal = bad, ill, wrongful,
disordered
micro = small
para = beyond, beside
peri = around

poly = many, multiple
post = after
pre = before, in front of
pseud(o) = false
re = again
retro = backward, be-
hind
sub = under, below
super = above, beyond,
over
supra = above
syn = together

The next group, which might be called the roots or combining forms, are at the center of words. They tend to denote
a relationship to a particular body part, usually an organ affected by a condition:

abdomin = abdomen,
stomach
adeno = gland
adip = fat
angi(o) = vessel (blood,
lymph)
cardi(o) = heart
col(o) = colon
colpo = vagina
culdo = from cul de
sac, meaning a
blind pouch or dead
end; in relationship
to rectouterine
space (the tissue be-
tween the apex of
the vagina and the
rectum)
cut = skin
cystido, cysto = bladder,
sac, cyst
cyto = cell
enter = intestine
gastr(o) = stomach
gyno = any female re-
productive organ
hema, hemato, hemo =
blood

hepat(o) = liver
hyster(o) = uterus
ile, ili = intestines,
lower abdomen
labi = lip
lact = milk
lipo = fat
lumbar = loin
mast = breast
men(o) = menstruation
metr(a) = uterus
myo = muscle
neur(o) = nerves
ophor = ovary
os = mouth, opening
ov = egg
phleb = vein
procto = anus, rectum
ren = kidney
sacr(o) = sacrum
salping = fallopian tube
ur(o) = urinary tract
uter(o) = uterus
vagin(o) = vagina
vas = vessel, duct
veno = vein
vesic = bladder
vulv(o) = vulva

Finally, there are the suffixes—the linguistic cabooses with
the rather unpleasant job here of specifying what has gone

wrong with the part designated by your prefix and combining form or root:

algia = pain

blast = a growth in its early stages

cele = tumor, hernia

cente = puncture

dynia = pain

ectomy = excision of, surgical removal of

itis = inflammation

lysis = freeing of

megaly = very large

oma = tumor, swelling

oscopy = looking at an organ or internal part

osis = disease, abnormal condition or process

ostomy = creation of an artificial opening

otomy = incision, cutting into

pathy = disease of, abnormality

plasty = reconstruct, formation of

rhage, rhagia, rrhage, rrhagia = bleeding

rhea, rrhea = flow, discharge

uria = urine (condition of, presence in)

Put them all together, and they spell "Huh?" But really, it isn't all that complicated. For example, say your impress-the-ladies gynecologist has run a series of tests and now informs you that you have dysmenorrhea. Consult the lists: prefix *dys* means painful or difficult; *men* means menstrual; *rrhea* means flow or discharge. Instead of being awed by his diagnosis, you realize that he's just tossing off a fancy word for menstrual cramps!

CHAPTER SIX

Keeping a Record

Getting Copies of Your Medical Records

eeping track of your medical history is important. You may want to obtain copies of your medical records for any number of reasons, including the following:

- To piece together a picture of your weight, blood pressure, cholesterol levels, or any other medical condition over time.
- To learn what is being said by professionals about you and the diagnosis and prognosis of your condition, particularly if you feel they are being reticent in giving you information about yourself.
- To see if there is misinformation or comments about you that could jeopardize your ability to obtain medical insurance or affect your treatment.
- If you believe your doctor has been negligent in your care, and plan to sue. (In this case, you may have already talked with a lawyer. If so, she will solicit your records.)

The medical records kept at your doctor's office usually include

- the medical history form you filled out when you first became a patient;
- information about any medical insurance you have;
- notes from every visit to this doctor, including findings during examination, your diagnosis, and medications prescribed;
- the doctor's personal notes about your condition, appearance, questions, comments or concerns, or anything else he cares to remember about you;
- copies of laboratory test results; and
- letters or other information from any consulting doctors.

Your medical records at a hospital consist of your medical chart for each hospitalization you've had at that hospital. The chart includes

- reports from various hospital departments—X ray, electrocardiogram (EKG), respiratory and rehabilitation services, and the like;
- various laboratory reports—urinalysis, cytology, hematology, and the like;
- doctors' notes on your progress, your history, and the findings of physical or mental exams;
- nurses' notes on your physical and mental condition;
- notes or letters from any consulting doctors brought in on your case; and
- various consent forms.

In almost every case, you are entitled to copies of your medical records, both physician and hospital files. However, the originals belong to the doctor or hospital.

Only a handful of states have passed laws to guarantee your right to copies of your medical records. Where there is no law supporting your right, there is also no law prohibiting you from having copies. Doctors and hospitals may tell you that it is illegal for you to have copies of your records. If this happens to you, ask them to recite chapter and verse of the particular law.

When requesting copies of your records, try the following procedure:

1. Contact the doctor or hospital and ask how to obtain copies of your records. Make note of whom you spoke to, the date and time, and what the person said.

2. Put your request in writing. Include your name, your patient ID number (if known), and the specific entry or file you want. Indicate your willingness to pay reasonable copying costs. You may also want to enclose a self-addressed, stamped envelope.

3. If your request is denied by telephone or ignored completely, have the provider put the denial in writing, citing the reason for refusal and any statute they claim prevents them from supplying records. Also have them include what appeal procedures may be available.

If you are still unable to obtain copies of your records, you may contact the patient representative at the hospital, or request a "friendly" physician to request a copy of your hospital records or the records at another doctor's office.

You can also obtain a court order from a magistrate or civil court. Consult with a lawyer to do this. You must be willing to persevere if you want copies of your medical records. Remember, the first step is always a request. If that is ignored, you may seek assistance from the courts.

Your Personal Medical Records

The following forms will help you keep track of

- a potential doctor's training and credentials;
- frequently used medical phone numbers;
- your gynecologic history;
- your risk factors based on your family's medical history;
- gynecological symptoms and breast tissue conditions;
- doctors' visits;
- major hospitalizations and test results;
- medications and side effects; and
- consent forms.

To best use these forms, make copies before you write on them. Keep your filled-in copies in a loose-leaf notebook, along with copies of doctor and hospital records and laboratory test results.

DOCTOR INFORMATION WORKSHEET

Name of Doctor	Doctor 1	Doctor 2	Doctor 3	Doctor 4
Private Practice Doctor				
Is this doctor accepting new patients?				
If "no," when will he/she accept new patients?				
Is this doctor an M.D. or Doctor of Osteopathy?				
Is this doctor board-certified in ob-gyn?				
Does this doctor provide get-acquainted visits?				
How much time will I be given on this visit?				
How much will it cost?				
Does this doctor publish a list of his/her fees?				
What is the cost of a regular office visit?				
What is the charge when the doctor makes a hospital visit?				
Is payment demanded at the time of service?				
Does this doctor permit a flexible payment schedule?				
Is this doctor's location convenient to where I live?				
Is public transportation to the doctor's office available?				
Is there adequate parking at the doctor's office?				
Is this doctor in a solo or group practice?				
Do patients have direct telephone access to the doctor?				
Are there specific call-in times? When?				
Does this doctor offer lab work and other services in the office?				
What is the cost of these services?				
Does this doctor have convenient office hours?				
Does this doctor have office hours on weekends?				

Will my medical insurance coverage be accepted?			
Will the doctor file all insurance claims?			
Does this doctor accept Medicare assignment?			
Do I have access to my medical records?			
Do I have access to a summary of my medical records?			
Will I receive copies of all lab tests ordered by the doctor?			
Where does the doctor have hospital privileges?			
Is this hospital my first choice?			

HMO-PPO Worksheet

Doctor's medical degree? (M.D. or D.O.)			
Is this doctor board-certified in ob-gyn?			
Years in practice?			
Years in the HMO-PPO?			
Hospital(s) used by HMO-PPO?			
Are these hospitals your first choice?			
Prevention-oriented, health-education materials available?			
Amount of time spent with patients? (During normal visit)			
Communicates well with patients?			
Available for telephone consultations?			
Specific times available?			
Refers to specialists within plan?			
Refers to specialists outside plan?			
Your special questions:			
Comments or notes:			

195

QUICK REFERENCE GUIDE

List All Your Medical Providers and Emergency Telephone Numbers			
Name	Specialty	Address	Telephone

Police / Fire / Ambulance	Telephone	Hospital	Telephone
Crisis Hot Lines	Telephone	Pharmacies	Telephone

196

YOUR GYNECOLOGICAL MEDICAL CHECKLIST	Date	Date	Date
Abnormal Pap smear			
Abnormal breast exam			
Abnormal pelvic exam			
Abortion			
Age began menstruating			
Average number of days in cycle			
Average length of period			
Birth control pills			
Bleeding between periods			
Breast biopsy			
Cervical biopsy			
Colposcopy			
DES exposure			
Endometrial biopsy			
Fragile bones			
Hormone replacement therapy			
IUD			
Menopause			
Miscarriage			
Painful breasts			
Painful intercourse			
Painful menstruation			
Premenstrual symptoms			
Pregnancies			
Sexual dissatisfaction			
Sexually transmitted diseases			
Tubal ligation			
Tumors—breast			
Tumors—uterus			
Tumors—ovaries			
Vaginal infections			
Other comments and notes:			

FAMILY GYNECOLOGIC/BREAST CANCER MEDICAL HISTORY

Name of Relative	Relationship	Disease/ Condition	Age at Diagnosis	Deceased

RECORD OF YOUR DAILY SYMPTOMS

By noting any symptoms of pain, swelling, or irregular bleeding each day of your monthly menstrual cycle, you can help your doctor to diagnose conditions such as endometriosis, premenstrual syndrome, or premenopause. Your symptoms might be pelvic pain, pain during intercourse, abdominal swelling, and the like. Descriptive terms might include sharp, dull, throbbing, nauseating, and so forth. Note if your pain is associated with exercise, stress, sexual activity, and such. Continue this checklist for as many months as it takes to get an accurate picture of your symptoms. Day one is the day you start your period.

Day of Cycle	Problems / Complaints / Symptoms	Action Taken

─────── *Your Personal Calendar Worksheet*

Women often wonder, "How can I remember how my breast tissue feels from one monthly BSE to the next?" Well, it's easier than you think. You can use the method that most doctors use—a diagram like this one.

Using this personal calendar worksheet you can chart any changes in your breasts every time you perform BSE. Label any areas as firm, soft, or with any description that you feel explains how the tissue feels. Then the next month you can compare what you feel with the prior month's diagram. Take this valuable record with you to your doctor's office.

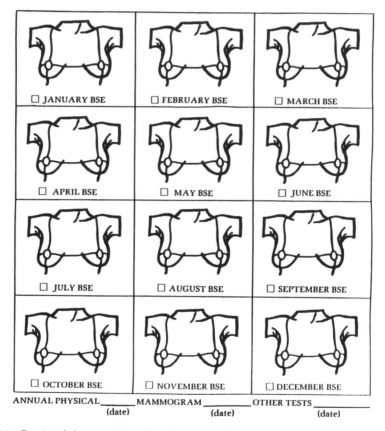

☐ JANUARY BSE   ☐ FEBRUARY BSE   ☐ MARCH BSE

☐ APRIL BSE   ☐ MAY BSE   ☐ JUNE BSE

☐ JULY BSE   ☐ AUGUST BSE   ☐ SEPTEMBER BSE

☐ OCTOBER BSE   ☐ NOVEMBER BSE   ☐ DECEMBER BSE

ANNUAL PHYSICAL_____ MAMMOGRAM _____ OTHER TESTS _____
         (date)   (date)   (date)

Note: Reprinted, by permission, from the booklet The Good News About Breast Cancer, *by WRS Group, Inc. (Waco, TX: WRS Group, Inc., 1991), p. 10. © 1991 by WRS Group, Inc.*

RECORD OF YOUR INDIVIDUAL VISITS

Date	Problems / Complaints / Symptoms	Diagnosis and Treatment

RECORD OF MAJOR HOSPITALIZATIONS

Date	Hospital	Doctor	Condition / Illness

RECORD AND RESULTS OF LABORATORY TESTS

Date	Lab Test	Results

RECORD OF PRESCRIPTION MEDICATIONS

Date	Medication	Doctor	Pharmacy	Side Effects

RECORD OF OVER-THE-COUNTER MEDICATIONS— INCLUDE VITAMINS AND MINERALS

Date	Medication	Date	Medication	Date	Medication

Consent to Operation or Other Special Procedure

PATIENT ___Jane Doe___ AGE __42__

DATE __11/1/91__ TIME __8:30__ (A.M)/P.M. CONSENT OBTAINED AT ___General Hospital___

(i.e., physician's office, hospital, etc.)

1. I authorize the performance upon ___myself___ of the following operation or procedure

(Myself or name of patient)

___myomectomy to remove fibroid tumors of the uterus using laseroscopy___.

(State nature and extent of operation)

① to be performed at The Hospital ~~under the direction of~~ by Dr. ___John Smith___ ~~and/or such associates~~ ~~and assistants as may be selected by him.~~ only for surgery, with assistance as needed.

2. The nature and purpose of the operation, referred to in Paragraph 1 hereof and the possible alternative methods of treatment have been explained to me by Dr. ___John Smith___ and to my complete satisfaction. No guarantee or assurance has been given by anyone as to the results that may be obtained.

3. I acknowledge that I have been afforded the opportunity to ask any questions with respect to the operation and any risks or complications thereto and to set forth, in the space provided below, any limitations or restrictions with respect to this consent:

② ___Under no circumstances is a hysterectomy to be performed.___

(If None, write "none")

___Ovaries and fallopian tubes are to remain intact.___

③ ~~4. I consent to the performance of operations, procedures, and treatment in addition to or different from those now contemplated as described above, whether or not arising from presently unforeseen conditions, which the above-named doctor or his associates or assistants may in his or their judgment consider necessary or advisable in my present illness.~~ *I do **not** consent.*

5. I understand that anesthesia shall be administered during this operation under the direction of the responsible physician.

④ ~~6. For the purpose of advancing medical education, I consent to the admittance of observers to the operating room.~~ *I do **not** consent.*

⑤ ~~7. I consent to the disposal by hospital authorities of any tissue or parts that may be removed.~~ *I do **not** consent.*

I CERTIFY THAT I HAVE READ AND FULLY UNDERSTAND THE ABOVE CONSENT, THAT THE EXPLANATIONS THEREIN REFERRED TO WERE MADE, THAT ALL BLANKS OR STATEMENTS REQUIRING INSERTION OR COMPLETION WERE FILLED IN, AND THAT INAPPLICABLE PARAGRAPHS, IF ANY, WERE STRICKEN BEFORE I SIGNED.

Signature of Patient ___Jane Doe___

Signature of Witness ___Paul Doe___

Witness to signature only

When a patient is a minor or incompetent to give consent:

Signature of person authorized to consent for patient _____

Relationship to patient _____

The foregoing consent was signed in my presence, and in my opinion the person did so freely with full knowledge and understanding.

Signature of Physician ___John Smith___

Signature of Witness ___Paul Doe___

Witness to signature only

204

The consent form reproduced here is similar to ones used in most hospitals and ambulatory surgical centers. Your signature on this form indicates that you have agreed to the performance of a specific procedure in a specific way, and that you have received adequate informational background. A different form should be completed before every procedure that you believe requires a consent contract, even if your doctor says it's unnecessary. Ask for one to be made up if your doctor doesn't offer one. Try to get a copy of the consent form to read in advance of your procedure or surgery.

Be sure that all the clauses are true and represent your beliefs before you sign the form. Be careful. The forms are filled with booby traps. If you need to alter, amend, or revise the form to fit your situation, do so. It is your right as a patient. Major changes in the form should have been discussed beforehand with your doctor. If this hasn't been done, it's possible you will be refused surgery until you and your doctor have straightened things out.

This consent form has been altered by the patient to suit her needs.

① By amending the form this way, Jane Doe makes clear that she has agreed that the major part of her surgery will be performed only by Dr. John Smith, not by any doctor-in-training under Dr. Smith's supervision. Her doctor may be assisted by others, however.

② Our patient makes it clear that she is not agreeing to a hysterectomy, or to removal of her ovaries or fallopian tubes under any circumstances. (Her doctor has already agreed to this.)

③ This clause in effect makes a mockery of the form and the entire consent process. Our patient eliminated it from the form.

④ Our patient wanted no one except those involved in her surgery to be present in the operating room. Some forms also have patients consenting to filming or videotaping of their operations. You might not want that.

⑤ Our patient felt this could leave the door open for cover-ups of botched or unnecessary surgery, so she did not consent to this.

Don't be rushed into signing the form. If you have trouble understanding it, request that someone from the hospital or surgical center's administrative office or legal department clarify the form or parts of it for you.

Informed consent is not and should not be a piece of paper, but an ongoing process, a partnership or information-sharing and trust between doctor and patient.

——— *Why Get a Mammogram?*

Mammograms can detect breast tumors in the earliest stage, when cure rates are highest. Consider the following:

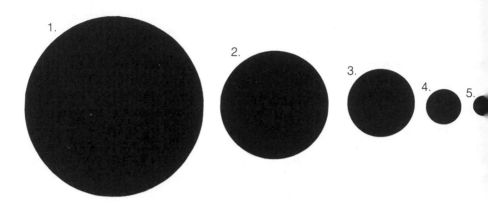

1. Average-size lump found by women untrained in BSE.
2. Average-size lump found by women practicing occasional BSE.
3. Average-size lump found by women practicing regular BSE.
4. Average-size lump found by first mammogram.
5. Average-size lump found by regular mammograms.

Note: Reprinted, by permission, from the booklet The Good News About Breast Cancer, *by WRS Group, Inc. (Waco, TX: WRS Group, Inc., 1991), p. 15. © 1991 by WRS Group, Inc.*

Epilogue

If you've read this far, and even if you've read only the parts that pertain to a particular problem, you've gotten the key point of this book: Ask questions. And get answers. Ask the kinds of questions about your medical care that elicit information that will help you to make responsible decisions.

You'll be much more likely to get medical care that is appropriate to your individual needs and concerns. And because you'll have played an active role in choosing that medical care, you'll feel less like a victim, and more in control. You'll be someone who has chosen, or not chosen, to have a hysterectomy or take replacement hormones—not someone whose doctor "said you had to." The truth is, whether or not you and your doctor discuss it, you always do have choices; and ultimately, you share with your doctor the responsibility for your health care.

The title of this book reflects its purpose and the way it can best serve you. This book is meant to be taken out into the world and used. Do take it with you to the gynecologist. Do refer to it during an office visit if necessary. Leave an extra copy in your gynecologist's waiting room, marked "For patient use." Donate a copy to your public library. Lend it to a needy friend. And do let us know how it has helped you.

Suggested Readings

Berkow, Robert (ed.). *The Merck Manual*, 15th ed. Rahway, N.J.: Merck & Co., 1989. (This book offers detailed descriptions of all but the most obscure ailments, a discussion of symptoms and signs, and diagnostic and therapeutic procedures.)

Boston Women's Health Book Collective. *The New Our Bodies, Ourselves*. New York: Simon & Schuster, 1984.

DiSaia, Philip, and William Creasman. *Clinical Gynecologic Oncology*, 3rd ed. St. Louis: C. V. Mosby Co., 1989. (Somewhat technical, but a good basic book on the diagnosis and treatment of all kinds of cancers of women's reproductive organs.)

Inlander, Charles B., and Karla Morales. *Getting the Most for Your Medical Dollar*. New York: Pantheon, 1990.

Inlander, Charles B., and Karla Morales. *Take This Book to the Obstetrician with You*. Reading, Mass.: Addison-Wesley, in press.

Inlander, Charles B., and Eugene I. Pavalon. *Your Medical Rights*. Boston: Little, Brown, 1990.

Inlander, Charles B., and Ed Weiner. *Take This Book to the Hospital with You*. Emmaus, Pa.: Rodale Press, 1985.

Inlander, Charles B., and Ed Weiner. *Take This Book to the Hospital with You: New and Revised*. New York: Pantheon, in press.

Keyser, Herbert H., M.D. *Women Under the Knife: A Gynecologist's Report on Hazardous Medicine*. New York: Warner Communications, 1984.

Napoli, Maryann. *Mammography Screening: A Decision-Making Guide*. New York: Center for Medical Consumers, 1990. (A pamphlet summarizing the latest research regarding the benefits and risks of mammography screening. For a copy of the guide, send $5 to 237 Thompson Street, New York, New York, 10012. Send $8 for the New

York City edition, which includes a listing of all facilities that have passed the state's Quality Assurance Program.

National Women's Health Network. *Taking Hormones and Women's Health: Choices, Risks, Benefits.* Washington, D.C.: National Women's Health Network, 1989.

Parsons, Langdon, M.D., and Sheldon Sommers, M.D. *Gynecology.* Philadelphia: W. B. Saunders, 1978. (A 1,600-page tome covering all aspects of gynecology, with many photos and drawings.)

Payer, Lynn. *How to Avoid a Hysterectomy.* New York: Pantheon, 1987.

Robin, Eugene D. *Matters of Life and Death.* New York: W. H. Freeman, 1984.

Scully, Diana H. *Men Who Control Women's Health.* Boston: Houghton Mifflin, 1980.

Todd, Alexandra Dundas. *Intimate Adversaries: Cultural Conflict Between Doctors and Women Patients.* Philadelphia: University of Pennsylvania Press, 1989.

Wolfe, Sidney M., M.D., and the Public Citizen Health Research Group with Rhoda Donlin Jones. *Women's Health Alert.* New York: Addison-Wesley, in press.

Glossary

Abdomen The part of the body between the chest and the pelvis; the belly. The abdominal cavity contains most of the body's digestive organs, among them the stomach and intestines. Also in this cavity, which is separated from the chest by the diaphragm, are the liver, gallbladder, spleen, and kidneys.

Adhesions Scar tissue that forms after infection, surgery, or curettage that can close off the cervix, make the sides of the uterus stick together, block the fallopian tubes, or constrict other pelvic organs and cause pain. Adhesion formation is particularly common in abdominal surgery; microsurgery techniques can minimize adhesions.

Ambulatory Walk-in, same-day, or outpatient (usually referring to surgery, and distinct from inpatient or hospital care).

Amniocentesis Withdrawal with a long needle of fluid from the sac surrounding a fetus for analysis.

Biopsy The removal of a portion of body tissue to examine microscopically and make a diagnosis. It is widely used to determine the status of growths that may be cancerous. An open biopsy is done by an incision through the skin. A needle biopsy or needle aspiration biopsy is done by inserting a needle through the skin into the area where tissue is to be taken. It's used to check breast lumps thought to be fluid-filled cysts. A punch biopsy uses a surgical instrument similar to a small paper punch to extract a plug of skin and tissue. It's used on surface lesions as may be found on the cervix, on the vulva, or in the vagina. (For *cone biopsy*, see CONIZATION.)

Catheterization The passage of a flexible surgical tube into an opening. Urinary catheterization refers to passage of a tube into the bladder to allow drainage of urine. It is a common cause of bladder infections.

Cauterization   The application of a caustic substance, a hot instrument, an electric current, or other agent to destroy diseased tissue. Cauterization might be used to remove venereal warts from the cervix or vagina.

Cervical intraepithelial neoplasm (CIN)   *Neoplasm* means "new and abnormal tissue growth," which may or may not be cancerous.

Intraepithelial means "among the cells" lining the cervix. This is a relatively new term used by pathologists to replace an older and less specific term, *dysplasia*, which simply means "abnormal development of cells."

Cervicitis   Inflammation of the cervix. (There are several types.)

Cervix   The neck of the uterus which extends into the upper part of the vagina; a fairly common site for cancer, and the area from which a Pap smear is taken.

Cesarean section   The surgical procedure in which the uterus is cut open to remove a fetus.

Chlamydia   Pronounced klah-mid-dee'-ah, a strange, viruslike, sexually transmitted bacteria that can cause severe pelvic inflammatory disease.

Colposcopy   A procedure that uses a magnifying instrument to examine the surface of the cervix for lesions, and to pinpoint the areas from which tissue will be taken for biopsy.

Conization   The surgical procedure in which a cone-shaped piece of tissue is cut out of the center of the cervix; used to diagnose or rule out the presence of invasive cancer. Also known as a *cone biopsy*.

Cryosurgery   Destruction of tissue by extreme cold. Cryosurgery often replaces cauterization today as a way to remove surface lesions.

Cul-de-sac   In gynecology, a "blind pouch" of tissue between the vagina and rectum that sometimes harbors endometriosis or tumors; it's examined by being felt through the rectum.

Cyst   A noncancerous, fluid-filled cavity or sac. In fibrocystic "disease" of the breast or benign breast condition, the breasts are riddled with cysts.

Cystitis   Inflammation of the urinary bladder.

Cystocele   A condition where the bladder bulges through the vaginal wall. Also known as a *cystic hernia*.

Danazol   Marketed in the United States as Danocrine, a synthetic hormone used to treat endometriosis. Derived from the male hormone testosterone, this drug stops menstruation and the hormonal peaks of ovulation, and dissolves small endometrial implants and may shrink larger ones.

DES (diethylstilbestrol) A synthetic hormone prescribed to three to six million pregnant women in the United States between 1941 and 1971, usually to prevent miscarriage. (The drug was never proven to do this.) DES has been found to cause abnormalities of the reproductive system and, in some cases, cancer at an early age. Women who know or suspect they've been exposed to DES should have a special pelvic and vaginal exam done by a doctor experienced with DES patients.

Diagnosis The determination of the nature of the case of a disease; the art of distinguishing one disease from another.

Dilation and curettage (D&C) A procedure in which the opening of the cervix is stretched, and a sharp spoon-shaped instrument (a curette) is inserted and used to scrape away the uterine lining. This procedure has been mostly replaced by techniques that use a flexible plastic tube and suction.

Dysplasia A term doctors often use to refer to possibly precancerous cells. It simply means "abnormal development of cells."

Ectopic pregnancy Development of a fertilized egg outside the uterus, usually in the fallopian tubes. Very painful, it often requires emergency surgical removal.

Endocervical curettage A process in which tissue is scraped from the endocervix, the opening in the cervix to the uterus. This is most often done as part of a cervical biopsy, after a Pap smear shows signs of abnormalities.

Endocrinology The study of the hormone-secreting organs (the endocrine system) in the body. This includes the study of the ovaries in women, and in men, the testicles.

Endometriosis A painful condition in which the endometrium, the tissue lining the uterus, migrates outside the uterus and grows on other organs within the abdomen.

Endometrium The tissue lining the uterus which responds to hormone levels and is shed every month as menstrual flow.

Estrogen A female hormone produced in the ovaries that is responsible for most feminine sex characteristics. Estrogen is used in birth control pills, to treat symptoms of menopause, and to prevent osteoporosis.

Estrogen receptor assay A test done on breast cancer tumors and other gynecological tumors immediately on removal to determine if, and how much, their growth is enhanced by the hormone estrogen. Women with estrogen-receptive tumors are often given estrogen-suppressing drugs.

Fallopian tubes   The tiny, muscular tubes that carry eggs from the ovaries to the body of the uterus. Scarred fallopian tubes are a common cause of infertility in women.

Fibroid tumors   Solid, usually benign tumors that grow on the outside, inside, or within the wall of the uterus (technically known as *leiomyomas* or *myomas*). They are a common reason gynecologists recommend hysterectomy, although fibroids can be treated by other means, and often don't require treatment.

Genitourinary   Pertaining to the area around the genitals and urinary tract.

Gonadotropin releasing hormone agonists   New drugs used in the treatment of endometriosis which inhibit ovarian function and lower estrogen levels.

Gynecologic oncologist   A gynecologist with special training in the treatment of cancer of women's reproductive organs.

Gynecologist   A medical doctor specializing in the treatment of diseases of women's reproductive organs.

Hematocrit   A measurement of the volume of red blood cells found in a certain amount of blood; used along with other factors to determine a woman's blood iron level.

Hemoglobin   The oxygen-carrying pigment found in red blood cells; used along with other factors to determine a woman's blood iron level.

Hormone replacement therapy (HRT)   The use of synthetic or naturally occurring hormones to replace those the body is no longer producing because of menopause or removal of the ovaries. HRT most often includes estrogen and progesterone, and sometimes male hormones known as androgens.

Human papilloma virus (HPV)   A large group of sexually transmitted viruses that cause all forms of venereal warts and lesions. Some types of this virus have been linked with cervical cancer.

Hysterectomy   The surgical removal of the uterus. There are a number of different kinds of hysterectomies, depending on how the operation is performed.

Hysteroscopy   A diagnostic and surgical procedure in which a thin, tubular viewing scope is inserted through the cervix into the uterus. It's used to look for internal uterine growths such as polyps or fibroid tumors.

Infertility   Diminished or absent capacity to produce offspring. The term does not denote complete inability to produce offspring, as does the term *sterility*. Primary infertility is that occurring in people who have never conceived; secondary infertility occurs in people who have previously conceived.

In situ   In place; cancer that has not yet spread.

Internist A medical doctor who specializes in the diagnosis and medical (as opposed to surgical) treatment of adults.

Intrauterine device (IUD) A form of contraception in which a small plastic piece is inserted into the uterus, with withdrawal string extending through the cervix into the vagina. Currently, only two kinds of IUD are available in the United States. IUDs have been associated with pelvic inflammatory disease and are not recommended for women who intend to have children in the future and/or who are not in a monogamous relationship.

In vitro fertilization *In vitro* means, literally, "in glass" or "observable in a test tube." The process of joining egg and sperm outside the body, in a laboratory-controlled environment, then injecting the newly fertilized egg into the mother's womb.

Laparoscopy Examination of the interior of the abdomen by means of a laparoscope, a thin metal viewing scope, which is inserted through a small incision. Laparoscopy is often done to diagnose endometriosis and other infertility problems.

Laser surgery The process of using a laser (a concentrated beam of light that can produce a tremendous amount of heat) to cut or otherwise destroy tissue. In the hands of a well-skilled surgeon, certain lasers have the advantage of being more precise and of causing less blood loss than traditional surgery with a knife.

Mammography The process of X-raying the breasts (mammary glands) to detect lumps or thickened tissue that could be cancerous.

Mastectomy The surgical removal of the breast. There are several different kinds of mastectomy.

Menopause The cessation of menstrual periods in women, usually occurring around age fifty. Surgically induced menopause is caused by the removal of the ovaries.

Menstruation The shedding through the vagina of the uterine lining, consisting of blood and tissue. Average cycle is twenty-eight days; average length of menstrual period, five days.

Microinvasive cancer Cancer that has just started to invade surrounding tissue, and that may still be treated by local removal.

Microsurgery Surgical techniques that use a microscope to incise and stitch tiny structures such as the fallopian tubes; also, refined surgical techniques that minimize bleeding and scarring.

Myomectomy The surgical removal of fibroid tumors from the uterus.

Oncology The study of cancer, especially tumors.

Oophorectomy Pronounced oh-for-rek'-tow-me, the surgical removal of one ovary; also called *ovariectomy*. Bilateral oophorectomy indicates removal of both ovaries.

Osteoporosis A condition in which the bones lose mass and become porous, resulting in weak bones that can fracture easily. Osteoporosis is most common in small-boned, light-skinned, sedentary women past the age of menopause.

Ovaries Olive-shaped glands connected by the fallopian tubes to the uterus which secrete estrogen, the main female hormone, and which, in fertile women, produce an egg each month.

Ovulation The process during which the ovary produces an egg.

Ovum The egg (cell) produced monthly in the ovaries.

Pap smear A test in which cells are scraped from the cervix, smeared on a glass slide, and examined under a microscope for signs of cancer or infection.

Pelvic inflammatory disease (PID) A serious, sexually transmitted infection of the uterus, fallopian tubes, and/or ovaries. PID can result in sterility. Symptoms of pelvic pain, fever, chills and pus-like vaginal discharge require a doctor's immediate attention.

Pelvis The lower portion of the trunk of the body, including the pelvic bones and those organs within the hip bones. In women, this includes the entire reproductive tract.

Pessary A plastic or metal ring or cap used to hold a fallen (prolapsed) uterus in place.

Primary care physician A person's only doctor, or the doctor a patient is most likely to see first for an illness.

Progesterone A female hormone secreted by the ovaries which causes changes in the endometrium that help to ensure pregnancy. Adequate levels of progesterone after ovulation, followed by a sharp drop in both progesterone and estrogen at the end of the menstrual cycle, lead to menstruation. Progesterone is used to correct abnormal bleeding in women near menopause; with estrogen for menopausal hormone replacement therapy; and sometimes as a treatment for premenstrual syndrome. Progestins are synthetic forms of progesterone.

Progesterone receptor assay A test done on breast cancer tumors and other gynecological tumors immediately on removal to determine if, and how much, their growth is enhanced by the hormone progesterone. Women with progesterone-receptive tumors are often given progesterone-suppressing drugs.

Prognosis A forecast as to the probable outcome of a disease; the prospects for recovery from a disease as indicated by the nature and symptoms of the case. The term is distinct from diagnosis.

Prolapse The falling down or sinking of an organ. In uterine prolapse, the uterus drops into the vagina. The bladder and rectum can also prolapse, sometimes bulging into the vagina. And, after a hysterectomy, the vagina can prolapse, caving in on itself.

Psychosomatic Bodily symptoms of psychic, emotional, or mental origin.

Radiologist A medical doctor who specializes in the use of radiation for diagnosis, especially in taking and interpreting X rays.

Radiotherapist A medical doctor who specializes in the treatment of disease, especially cancer, by means of radiation.

Radiotherapy The treatment of disease, especially cancer, by means of radiation.

Sacrum The triangular bone near the bottom of the spine, usually formed by five fused spinal vertebrae that are wedged between the hip bones.

Speculum A duckbill-shaped instrument inserted into the vagina and locked open that allows one to view the cervix and to insert and withdraw instruments without touching the sides of the vagina.

Toxic shock syndrome A rare disease, believed to be caused by staph bacteria, that causes high fever, vomiting, and sometimes death. (Five percent of all women who get toxic shock syndrome die.) In women, the disease has been associated with the use of tampons. It has been estimated that each year six to seventeen of every one hundred thousand menstruating women and girls will get toxic shock syndrome. To minimize your risks, use the least absorbent tampon needed to meet your needs and alternate with sanitary napkins.

Tubal ligation A process of sterilization in which the fallopian tubes are tied to prevent egg and sperm from uniting.

Ultrasound The visualization of deep structures in the body by recording the echoes of sound waves directed into the tissue. Also known as *sonography*, the technique is used to examine the unborn fetus and to detect fluid-filled cysts on the ovaries or in the breasts.

Urethra The canal conveying urine from the bladder to the outside of the body. In women, the urethra is about one inch long.

Urinary incontinence The inability to control the flow of urine, resulting in leaking of urine at inappropriate times.

Uterus The hollow, muscular, pear-shaped organ in women in which a fertilized egg becomes embedded and in which the developing fetus is nourished.

Vacuum aspiration A procedure in which suction is used to draw out fluid and tissue. A vacuum aspiration of the uterus removes the endometrial lining and other contents, and may be used as a means of terminating an early pregnancy.

Vagina The muscular canal leading from the vulva to the cervix.

Vaginitis Infection of the vagina, caused by any number of bacteria and microorganisms. Most common are yeast infections (also called *Candida, monilia,* and *fungus; trichomonas vaginalis* (*trich*); and *gardnerella*).

Vulva The region of the external genitalia of a woman.

Xeromammography A certain type of X ray of the breast that uses a photoelectric rather than film screen process. Although it provides sharper images than the film screen method, xeromammography requires more radiation, so it's not as widely used as film screen mammography.

Additional

Resources

The following organizations have a special interest in women's health concerns and may be able to offer specific assistance with a particular problem:

American Board of Medical Specialties (ABMS)
One Rotary Center, Suite 805
Evanston, Illinois 60201
1-800-776-CERT, 1-312-491-9091

Call this board's toll-free number (1-800-776-CERT), to find out if a particular doctor is ABMS-board-certified. The ABMS also offers a pamphlet—"Which Medical Specialist for You?"—that describes each medical specialty and provides the address for each specialty's certifying medical board.

American Board of Obstetrics and Gynecology (ABOG)
4225 Roosevelt Way, N.E., Suite 305
Seattle, Washington 98105
1-206-547-4884

Can tell you if a particular gynecologist is ABOG-certified, an active candidate for the board, or certified in a subspecialty—gynecologic oncology, maternal and fetal care, or reproductive endocrinology.

American Cancer Society
(Look in the white pages of your phone book for the office nearest you.)

Provides information, guidance, and referrals to agencies and community resources; home care items; transportation to and from local medical appointments; and support groups.

American College of Obstetricians and Gynecologists
409 12th Street, S.W.
Washington, D.C. 20024
1-202-638-5577

Call or write to check board certification of a gynecologist or for a list of their free patient information pamphlets.

American College of Radiology
1891 Preston White Drive
Reston, Virginia 22091
Attn.: Mammography Accreditation Program
1-703-648-8900

Call or write for the name and location of the mammography center nearest you that is accredited by this organization.

American Fertility Society
2140 11th Avenue South, Suite 200
Birmingham, Alabama 35205-2800
1-205-933-8494

Provides referrals to doctors with an interest in treating infertility and a list of free patient information publications.

American Osteopathic Association
142 East Ontario
Chicago, Illinois 60611-286·:
1-800-621-1773

Provides information on osteopathic medicine in general; can tell you whether a particular osteopathic hospital is accredited by their organization and whether an osteopathic gynecologist is board-certified.

American Osteopathic Board of Obstetrics and Gynecology
Ohio University School of Osteopathic Medicine
Grosvenor Hall, West 064
Athens, Ohio 45701
1-614-593-2239

Checks board certification of osteopathic gynecologists.

Boston Women's Health Book Collective
Box 192
West Somerville, Massachusetts 02114
1-617-625-0271

A medical consumer/membership organization that maintains a consumer health library, open to the public two days a week, and publishes books and brochures on women's health issues. Send a business-size self-addressed stamped envelope for a list of publications, services, and current activities.

Cancer Information Service of the National Cancer Institute
1-800-4-CANCER

Provides a free cancer information service staffed by trained counselors. Addresses a wide variety of needs of cancer patients, including specific details on any of 150 types of cancer; referrals to hospitals; support groups; information on financial aid; and access to the Physician's Data Query (PDQ) information base, a service that offers information on standard and experimental cancer treatments.

Center for Medical Consumers
237 Thompson Street
New York, New York 10012
1-212-674-7105

Provides a medical library and publishes *HealthFacts*, a newsletter that clearly presents controversial health care issues. Write for a list of topics covered in back issues.

DES Action
National office:
1615 Broadway
Oakland, California 94612
1-415-465-4011

East Coast office:
Long Island Jewish-Hillside Medical Center
New Hyde Park, New York 11040
1-516-826-5060

Provides information to women concerned about the use of DES or other hormones during pregnancy. Refers to doctors nationwide with expertise in DES-exposed health problems.

Endometriosis Association
Box 92187
Milwaukee, Wisconsin 53202
1-800-992-ENDO (U.S.), 1-800-426-2END (Canada)
1-414-962-8972 in Wisconsin or for business calls

Provides information on the latest medical and self-help treatment for endometriosis; referrals to doctors specializing in treatment; and help starting local support groups. Maintains a toll-free crisis-call service with trained counselors and a speaker's bureau.

Gynecologic Laser Society
6900 Grove Road
Thorofare, New Jersey 08086
1-800-257-8290, 1-609-848-1000

Provides referrals to doctors with an interest in gynecologic laser surgery; its 1,100 members include physicists, chemists, and equipment manufacturers. No training requirements to join.

HERS Foundation (Hysterectomy Educational Resources and Services)
422 Bryn Mawr Avenue
Bala Cynwyd, Pennsylvania 19004
1-215-667-7757
Offers support and counseling to women who have had or are contemplating hysterectomy. Extremely antihysterectomy.

Joint Commission on the Accreditation of Health Care Organizations
One Renaissance Boulevard
Oakbrook Terrace, Illinois 60181
1-708-916-5600
Can tell you if a particular hospital or ambulatory care center is accredited by their organization.

National Women's Health Network
1325 G Street, N.W.
Washington, D.C. 20005
1-202-347-1140
A national consumer membership/networking organization that works to influence government health policies. Write for a free directory of topics and a one-page brief on your particular health concern. Packets of forty to fifty pages of specific information are available for $5.

Planned Parenthood
(Look in the white pages of your phone book for the office nearest you.)
Provides gynecological exams, birth control and abortion information, AIDS testing, and treatment for sexually transmitted diseases on a pay-what-you-can basis. Confidential and available to anyone of any age.

RESOLVE
5 Water Street
Arlington, Massachusetts 02174
1-800-662-1016
A self-help group with chapters around the country that provide referrals, support, and information on infertility.

Index